LASTINGNESS

Also by Nicholas Delbanco

Fiction

The Count of Concord

Spring and Fall

The Vagabonds

What Remains

Old Scores

In the Name of Mercy

The Writers' Trade, & Other
Stories

About My Table, & Other
Stories

Stillness

Sherbrookes

Possession

Small Rain

Fathering

In the Middle Distance

News

Consider Sappho Burning

Grasse 3/23/66

The Martlet's Tale

Nonfiction

Anywhere Out of the World: Travel, Writing, Death

The Countess of Stanlein Restored: A History of the Countess of
Stanlein ex-Paganini Stradivarius Violoncello of 1707

The Lost Suitcase: Reflections on the Literary Life

Running in Place: Scenes from the South of France

The Beaux Arts Trio: A Portrait

Group Portrait: Conrad, Crane, Ford, James, & Wells

Books Edited

Literature: Craft and Voice (with A. Cheuse)

The Hopwood Lectures: Sixth Series

The Hopwood Awards: 75 Years of Prized Writing

The Sincerest Form: Writing Fiction by Imitation

The Writing Life: the Hopwood Lectures, Fifth Series

Talking Horse: Bernard Malamud on Life and Work
(with A. Cheuse)

Speaking of Writing: Selected Hopwood Lectures

Writers and Their Craft: Short Stories and Essays on the Narrative
(with L. Goldstein)

Stillness and Shadows (two novels by John Gardner)

LASTINGNESS

The Art of Old Age

NICHOLAS DELBANCO

GRAND CENTRAL
PUBLISHING

NEW YORK   BOSTON

Pictured on the front cover from left to right: (first row) Johann Sebastian Bach, Johann Wolfgang von Goethe, Georges Sand, Thomas Hardy, Rembrandt van Rijn; *(second row)* Henry Moore, Giuseppe Tomasi di Lampedusa, Pablo Picasso, Ralph Vaughan Williams, Henri Matisse; *(third row)* Leonardo da Vinci, Georgia O'Keeffe, Friedrich Holderlin, Giuseppe Verdi, Franz Joseph Haydn.

Grand Central Publishing
Hachette Book Group
237 Park Avenue
New York, NY 10017

www.HachetteBookGroup.com

Printed in the United States of America

First Edition: January 2011
10 9 8 7 6 5 4 3 2 1

Grand Central Publishing is a division of Hachette Book Group, Inc. The Grand Central Publishing name and logo is a trademark of Hachette Book Group, Inc.

Library of Congress Cataloging-in-Publication Data
Delbanco, Nicholas.
    Lastingness : the art of old age / Nicholas Delbanco. — 1st ed.
      p. cm.
    ISBN 978-0-446-19964-3
  1. Creative ability in old age.   2. Creation (Literary, artistic, etc.)   3. Older artists.   4. Older people—Psychology.   I. Title.
    BF724.85.C73D45 2011
    155.67'2—dc22

                                                                2010013874

For my Granddaughters

Anna Delbanco Shalom
&
Penelope Aurora Stoller
&
Rosalie Delbanco Shalom

With My Lasting Love

Portions of this book have been published, in slightly different versions, in the following:

Chapter 1, *The Boston Review*, vol. 32, 2007
Chapter 2, *Conjunctions*, 51, 2008
Chapter 4, *Salmagundi*, nos. 160–161, Fall/Winter, 2008–09
Chapter 5, *Ninth Letter*, Spring/Summer, 2009
Chapter 6, *Michigan Quarterly Review*, Summer, 2009
Chapter 7, *The Review of Contemporary Fiction*, vol. XXVIII, Fall, 2008
Chapter 8, *Salmagundi*, nos. 166–167, Spring/Summer, 2010

In the course of these last years, several friends and colleagues have read and responded to portions of this—or the entire—work: Charles Baxter, William Bolcom, George Bornstein, Alan Cheuse, Daniel Herwitz, Laurence J. Kirshbaum, Elizabeth Kostova, James Landis, Suzanne Levine, Richard Miller, Robert Rosenberg, Douglas Trevor, and Jon Manchip White. Singly and together, they have provided me with expert advice, and I am grateful to each. My student Carolyn Dekker proved far more competent than I in the apparatus of scholarship, and I owe part of the research and all of the footnotes to her expert help. Andrea Beauchamp, the assistant director of the Hopwood Awards Program, helped me identify the photographs so central to the text; Sara Weiss of Grand Central Publishing helped me to procure them and was tireless in last-stage detail work; Bob Castillo oversaw this book's production with his usual exacting eye and welcome expertise. My agent Gail Hochman (Brandt & Hochman, Inc.) and editor Jamie Raab (Grand Central Publishing) were, as always, crucial to the enterprise and supportive from the start. The first and lasting witness, as well as closest reader, remains my wife, Elena. To all of you, deep thanks.

CONTENTS

INTRODUCTION

Grow old along with me.
The best is yet to be,
The last of life, for which the first was made:
Robert Browning, *Rabbi Ben Ezra*

America grows older yet stays focused on its young. Whatever hill we try to climb, we're over it by fifty—and should that hill involve entertainment or athletics we're finished long before. There are exceptions to this rule, of course, but supermodels and newscasters, ingénues and football players all yield to the harsh tyranny of time. They turn on Fortune's wheel. Look what happens to the overnight sensation or pick of the week or fashion of the season or rookie of the year. First novels have a better chance of being noticed than a fourth or fifth. Although we're aging as a nation we don't do it willingly: The face-lift and the tummy-tuck are—against the law of gravity—on a commercial rise.

Still, we join the workforce older; we get married and have children older; we live, the actuaries tell us, longer than ever before. In Sun City or Las Vegas, the retired "golden codgers"—in William Butler Yeats's phrase—rule the commercial roost. And if younger is better it doesn't appear that youngest is best; we want our teachers, doctors, generals, and presidents to have reached a certain age. Our oldest elected chief executive, Ronald Reagan, famously quipped he wouldn't hold his opponent's youth against him. In context after context and contest after contest, we're more than a little conflicted about elders of the tribe; when is it right to honor them, and when to say "Step aside"?

This book is about tribal elders in the world of art. What interests me is lastingness: how it may be attained. For obvious reasons, this has become a personal matter; I published my first novel in 1966 and very much hope to continue. Too, such hope feels representative: a "generational" problem in both senses of the word. An ever-growing number of Americans are middle-aged or elderly; no natural catastrophe has thinned our swelling ranks. And the habit of creation does not die, so there are more who paint the sunset or take piano lessons or hunt the perfect end-rhyme at day's end. Our generation, like all others, yearns to produce some something that continues—and the generative impulse, when artistic, lingers on.

Yet it's a daunting proposition. To try to fashion work that might last more than a season is to recognize how hard it is to make a thing of beauty be "a joy forever"— that proud boast of a poet who died at twenty-five. John Keats tricked time; few can. (Mistakenly if modestly, he further claimed that his own epitaph should read: "Here lies One Whose Name was writ in Water.") There are pitfalls and pratfalls abounding; much can and does go wrong. Late style only rarely consists of advance, even when we're dealing, as one critic has described it, with "the senile sublime."[1]

So what does cause some artists just to fade away, and why is it that others soldier on? This introduction's epigraph comes at least partly tongue-in-cheek; "the last of life" is not routinely thought of as "the best." There are instances of quick success that lead to later failure—incandescent personalities who flare or gutter out. Some die too soon to confront diminution; others begin their work late. Still others remain at the easel or desk till exhaustion trumps exuberance and the whole system shuts down.

Issues of physical health and life expectancy enter in as well; what does it mean to be old in the twenty-first century as opposed to the sixteenth? (For those who suffer rapid loss—a stroke, a debilitating illness—the problem is a very different one. Yet my intention is, as much as possible, to leave to one side the complicating factors of physical collapse.) Late-stage creative personalities no doubt confront the human condition in ways analogous to those who deal with it from the ninth tee or nursing homes, but their response takes form in the concert hall or on the canvas or page. They leave evidence behind of having grappled with mortality, and—once mortality has claimed them—the evidence remains.

In these pages I consider what's been left behind: testimonials we hear and see and read. When that act of witnessing is offered up as language, what wording do we have that best describes old age? The late self-portraits of Rembrandt and the final songs of Richard Strauss are manifestly not the same as those produced while young. Which challenges continue and which ones are new?

●   ●   ●

All through the journey of this book, I weighed anchor in deepwater harbors. The metaphor feels strained but apt; "the journey of this book" has proved a task of navigation at least as much as destination. At project's start I thought that to advance one's art as time went on was seldom possible. The more I studied it, however, the more examples I unearthed of excellent work near or at career's end. This should not have been surprising; many of our culture's icons—from Sophocles to Michelangelo—lived for a very long time. And the trend will surely continue; as our population ages, its artists do the same.

Each time I picked a subject I felt a sense of loss. When writing of the painter Claude Monet, for instance, I found myself thinking: Why not such other elder artists as Arp? Bonnard? Chagall? Chardin? Degas? De Kooning? Kokoschka? Mantegna? Michelangelo? Renoir? Rouault? Tintoretto? Titian? Zurbarán? So the process of selection was a process of exclusion; this could be an omnibus volume yet remain a surface-scratch.

Further, the legion of old masters "elsewhere" is not within my ken. I don't doubt there are dancers in India, ceramists in Peru, woodworkers in Namibia whose work grows resplendent as they grow old. I do not doubt it but am unable to discuss it, and the artists and artificers of other crafts and cultures are—regretfully, respectfully—left out.

For a related reason, I focus on the dead. The verdict is not in on those whose work remains in progress; such judgment is provisional as well as incomplete.

But here is one such judgment. The stamp of personality is always case specific; what counts within the general rubric are individual markings. No fingerprint or snowflake is precisely like another, yet the category—*fingerprint, snowflake*—pertains. As these pages will attempt to show, when the category can be labeled *creative achievement in old age*, a pattern does emerge.

With very few exceptions the figures I here profile lived till seventy or older; most had known early success. All remained productive forces in their "sunset years." We're not talking about secret elixirs or monkey glands or Ponce de León's fabled quest; it's not as if they stumbled on youth's fountain or remained preternaturally agile. But there does seem some sort of common denominator, some stubborn refusal to retire or let well enough alone. The men and women I discuss therefore form a kind of cadre—whether they were working in the near or distant past. For reasons of economy I limit myself to literature, music, and the visual arts; somewhere in this haystack lies the needle, *lastingness*.

I hope to uncover it here.

CHAPTER ONE

Enemies of Promise

"You are old, Father William," the young man said,
  "And your hair has become very white;
And yet you incessantly stand on your head—
  Do you think, at your age, it is right?"

"In my youth," Father William replied to his son,
  "I feared it might injure the brain;
But, now that I'm perfectly sure I have none,
  Why, I do it again and again."

                      Lewis Carroll, "Father William"

Young people draw. They make up stories. They beat drums. Alive to the delights of clay and paper, children clap their hands and dance. That art starts as expressive play is widely understood by now; why some adults choose to continue with their lifelong playful gaming is less clear. Some call it "divine inspiration"; others are less flattering and urge artists to grow up. In *The Critic As Artist* (1891), Oscar Wilde proclaimed, "It is through Art, and through Art only, that we can realize our perfection; through Art and Art only that we can shield ourselves from the sordid perils of actual existence."[1] In the same year, and without the capital letter, he averred, "All art is quite useless."[2]

The creative impulse may well be strongest early on, before sex and getting and spending stake their own claims on attention. The child pressing down on a crayon or blowing through a tin kazoo will soon enough elect instead to play baseball or in bed. But there are those who cannot close the costume box or leave off telling stories or producing graven images and a joyful noise. These artists, if precocious, may flourish in their teenage years and make an original statement in their twenties; talent will be with them from the start.

And if there be a stereotype of the creative artist—particularly since the Romantic period—it tends to be of someone wild-haired, wide-eyed, *young*. John Keats died at twenty-five, Percy Bysshe Shelley at thirty, and George Gordon, Lord Byron made it to the ripe old age of thirty-six. In our present time the young performer—think of Kurt Cobain, James Dean, Jimi Hendrix, Janis

Joplin—is most adored when most at risk; the reckless-
ness that wrecked them had always been part of the act.
The common denominator here has to do with exuberance, an explosive energy that can become implosive;
these youthful talents share a sense that there's no point
in planning for tomorrow.

But for people in their seventies—not to mention their eighties and nineties—the future is a finite
thing and what's extensive is tradition: the long reach
of the past. It's not, I think, an accident that aging artists turn with invigorated interest to the work of predecessors or that they choose to revisit their own early
work. "Tomorrow and tomorrow and tomorrow" no
longer creeps in "petty pace from day to day" but with a
slow-motion rush. And to the extent that they manage
their time, the elderly must "pace" themselves in a different fashion than do the extravagant young. According to the *Oxford English Dictionary*, "lastingness" can be
defined as "the quality of being lasting; continuance;
duration; permanence. Also: durability, constancy, perseverance." The marathon and the hundred-yard dash
are very different things.

My title could pertain to both, since those who
sprint may well establish records that endure. But the
word's secondary meanings—"lastingness" as "durability, constancy, perseverance"—are increasingly at issue,
since there are more creative personalities at work in

what would once have seemed like great old age. White-haired Father William can stand on his head and yet sound better humored than the young man his son. The nonagenarian is no longer *extra*-ordinary, the centenarian no freak. The composer Elliott Carter celebrated his centenary in 2008 with a performance of new music. The artist-caricaturist Al Hirschfeld died at ninety-nine in 2003, the poet Stanley Kunitz in 2006 at one hundred; both were working near the end. To have been born in America in the twentieth century is to be part of a society longer lived than any previous; retirement now consists of decades and not years. And for those who don't choose to retire—who continue to wield pen or brush—a distant view is inescapable, no matter how close-watched the scene.

• • •

Throughout this book, though sparingly, I'll use the first-person pronoun, for there's no point pretending my interest in the subject is impersonal. Rather, it feels close to home. When I was twenty (thirty, forty, even fifty) the downward arc of a career seemed a problem for others to solve. Now, predictably enough, what I have come to admire are skills of continuity, consistency, and power-in-reserve. The men and women with whom this study deals all seem to have considered "the quality of being lasting."

It isn't a matter of mere endurance; many things

repeat themselves that we wish might end. It isn't a matter of shifting one's ground or starting over for novelty's sake. Rather, I find myself thinking of the painter Pierre-Auguste Renoir—so crippled by arthritis that he could not grasp the brush but had it wedged between his fingers—still poised above the canvas, squinting, jabbing at the image, adding color bit by bit. Or Arturo Toscanini, still ruthless in rehearsal, insisting that his orchestra play their *sostenuto* correctly and get intonation right. Or Johann Wolfgang von Goethe lying on his deathbed and asking for "More light…"

My father, Kurt Delbanco, kept Goethe's *Farbenlehre*—a study of chromatics—by his bedside in old age. Born in the city of Hamburg in 1909, my father fled from Hitler's Germany to England, and in the late 1940s came to America. A businessman by perceived necessity—my mother's expectations, and those of his three sons, were large—he had a lifelong interest in the visual arts. Both a collector and art dealer, he painted and made sculptures with a near obsessive passion; always I remember him with sketch pad and pencils, with tin-snips and hacksaw and easel and brush.

My father was a more than a Sunday painter; his oil portraits were acquired by such institutions as Harvard College, the National Portrait Gallery, and the Museum of the City of New York. He had one-man shows in Manhattan and elsewhere, but never attained full professional status, never quite broke out or through. This troubled him; he had dreams of being "discovered"—a kind of Grandpa Moses—in his tenth decade. At ninety-eight he continued to say, "A painting a day keeps the doctor away" and bend to his coloring book. The last time I saw him—on November 14, 2007—we talked about Francisco Goya, the artistic and commercial value of *Los Caprichos* and *Desastras de la Guerra;* he died two days thereafter, in his peaceful sleep.

My father-in-law, Bernard Greenhouse, is "only" ninety-four. World famous as a cellist—as soloist, chamber musician, and teacher—he owns the Countess of Stanlein ex-Paganini Stradivarius violoncello of 1707. I wrote a book about that instrument, as well as one on the Beaux Arts Trio, the chamber-music ensemble of which he was a founding member. So I have spent my married life observing a musician many thousands have applauded and still hear on recordings. Greenhouse was a student of Pablo Casals and like his teacher must confront the loss of physical agility and a performer's competence. Nowadays his public appearances consist of master classes; he does not play in concert, for the cello is a demanding taskmistress; strength fades. Since his eyesight no longer permits him to read music, he relies on memory, and his repertoire cannot enlarge. Still, every morning in his bathrobe, he blows on his fingers and picks up bow and cello and practices a Bach suite or a passage from Schumann or Brahms. An old man when he walks or shaves, he seems much younger when he sits to play or teach; there's an energy engendered by the task at hand, and only when he stands once more does he display his age.

These paired examples feel, in the root sense, familial: familiar, close to home. The men and women I will focus on are someone else's relatives, but they seem to me exemplary of a related set of challenges. My father said, a short while before his final illness, "I am not dying yet. But I am more ready for death than for life." My father-in-law, six years younger, still hungers to make music and for the ensuing applause. Those who admire such hunger call it "a force of nature"; those who think it less than seemly would counsel withdrawal instead. But in either case the act itself—of painting or playing the cello—became a source of vitality and not a drain thereof; both men shed years while engaged in their craft. And I find myself, while listening or watching (or sitting down each dawn to write), aware of the yield of old habit: how inspiriting it is to keep to a routine. If nothing else it offers up the comforts of continuity: As Father William tells his son, *I do it again and again.*

• • •

Lady Luck has much to do with this. Simply in terms of the number of throws, she blows on the old artist's dice.

There's the luck of robust health or available medical treatment; Mozart, Mendelssohn, and Schubert would have lived longer today. There's the luck of time and place; Rupert Brooke and Wilfred Owen, killed in the First World War, might well have extended their poetry's reach. To take a random sampling of painters dead before the age of forty—Masaccio, Caravaggio, Giorgione, and Raphael in the Italian Renaissance; Seurat, Lautrec, and Van Gogh in nineteenth-century France—is to recognize how many of our masters died while young. This is a commonplace, nearly, of *la vie bohème* and brilliant youth; disease and poverty and war are part of the scenario, and for every name that's known there are no doubt a hundred who died in anonymity because their luck was bad.

In the *Greek Anthology*, a collection of fragments from classical Greece, an epitaph encapsulates this elegiac yearning and dream of longer life:[3]

> In my nineteenth year the darkness drew me down.
> And ah, the sweet sun!
>
> (tr. Dudley Fitts)

Imagine for a moment that Edgar Allan Poe was committed to a clinic and there detoxified; imagine Stephen Crane, Franz Kafka, Katherine Mansfield, and Robert Louis Stevenson cured of consumption or the list of those with syphilis restored by penicillin; imagine Jean-Michel Basquiat and Egon Schiele—dead at twenty-eight—or Théodore Géricault—dead at thirty-three—somehow painting through their seventies and you'll see how much art history depends on sheer good fortune. Had François Villon *not* been condemned to the gallows or Christopher Marlowe been murdered in a tavern or Hart Crane grown suicidal, much of the canon might change. It's fine to think of Ludwig von Beethoven with a hearing aid or Virginia Woolf on antidepressants or thousands of soon-to-be-slaughtered twenty-year-old soldiers redeemed by armistice; if fate had been a little kinder or the appointment in Samarra missed it's fine to imagine additional work—another triptych, symphony, or novel to revere. Had "brilliant youth" enlarged to age just think what could be added to our culture's treasure trove.

But all such speculation is, of course, beside the point; we cannot know. What we have is what they left. What they did is what we have. And quite possibly a longer life would not entail artistic growth; Beethoven with his hearing fixed or Woolf in an affable Zoloft haze might not have managed to produce their great wrenching and pain-suffused work. The chapters that follow deal with extended careers, not the romance of early achievement; this book considers what happens to artists who endure. The twenty- and thirty- and forty-year-olds deserve a separate hearing; whatever problems they encounter do not include those of old age.

• • •

Of those who must prepare themselves for the second half of existence, Carl Jung observes:[4]

> Thoroughly unprepared we take the step into the afternoon of life; worse still, we take this step with the false assumption that our truths and ideals will serve us as hitherto. But we cannot live the afternoon of life according to the program of life's morning; for what was great in the morning will be little at evening, and what in the morning was true will at evening have become a lie.

We cannot know what lasts or will outlast us; we nonetheless prepare our work for strangers—viewers, listeners, and readers we may never meet. If the work is good enough, some of those strangers inhabit the future and are now unborn. "Continuance, duration, permanence" in this regard have more to do with the response of others than the stimulus provided; it's the reception of the piece and not its production that counts. But to the aging writer, painter, or musician the process can signify more than result; it no longer seems as important that the work be sold. So "lastingness" implies a doubled meaning in and for an artist's legacy; it's what gets left behind.

This is a crucial doubling, and germane throughout this book. It may well be true that needlepoint and crossword puzzles forestall the aging process, but I'm not writing about the therapeutic value of art or its function in consciousness raising. With only a few exceptions, the work here discussed has proved of lasting value in the estimation of *others*—those readers, viewers, listeners who receive it later on.

Therefore I will focus on the artist faced each day—each morning in the mirror—with the physical fact of decline. And since prose fiction is the discipline with which I'm most familiar, I'll start with this specific instance of the more general trend. The novelist is not exempt from the vagaries of fashion, neither from the loss of talent nor the shifting ground of recognition. Here, too, the field is littered with once lucky men and women ripe for the plucking—writers who flourished early on and who (disabled by injuries, alcohol, drugs, bitterness, insanity, inertia, an excess of intelligence, an adleaven of stupidity, a wasting disease, great wealth, great poverty, too much renown, too little, self-doubt, self-confidence, you name it) failed to continue. There's no obvious reason why this should hold true—why writers can't improve with age—but it's the rule, not exception, that most of the important work transpires early on.

If your expertise is basketball or ballet you understand, I would imagine, how early success is crucial and the chances of improvement at, say, thirty or fifty are slim. If you've not made the major leagues of piano playing or tennis or, as some suggest, theoretical physics by the age of forty, you're consigned to the bush leagues for life. Yet this needn't be the case for writers of prose fiction—whose subject, after all, is the wide range of human endeavor and not merely childhood or youth. Why should it seem so difficult to substitute endurance for enthusiasm, to temper ambition with artistry; what are, in Cyril Connolly's fine phrase, the "enemies of promise" that keep us from achieving the best work at the end?

First, a distinction to draw. F. Scott Fitzgerald died believing himself a has-been, but the books he wrote near the close of his life—*Tender Is the Night* and the unfinished *Last Tycoon*—easily outstrip, and today outsell, those almost-forgotten novels *(This Side of Paradise* and *The Beautiful and Damned)* that brought him early success. Herman Melville's *Typee* and *Omoo* established the career; his book about a whale was a commercial and critical disaster that now bestrides the narrow world of fiction like a Colossus. The work of Henry James is much more widely purchased at the present moment than to his disappointment held true for the texts while he lived. These are well-worn examples and familiar reversals. We've grown accustomed to "the cackle of the unborn about the grave,"[5] and the way a final verdict rarely upholds a first.

More appropriate to my discussion is that astonishing novella *Billy Budd,* written when Melville was old and ill and forgotten: a nearly perfect work of art produced, as it were, at the end. Thomas Mann did much the same, returning—decades after he'd first abandoned the project as unmanageable—to *Confessions of Felix Krull.* In our own time there are candidates. The novelists Penelope Fitzgerald and Harriet Doerr published no creative writing till their sixties; their fictions from the outset were mature. Peter Matthiessen in his eighties earned the National Book Award for revising a trilogy of novels he had published long before; in her ninth decade Doris Lessing received the Nobel Prize for Literature she continues to produce. The final novels of Wallace Stegner and recent books by Alice Munro, Philip Roth, and William Trevor are at least as prepossessing as their early texts.

• • •

Every artist has been made a gift but the offer is provisional and can be retracted. All must be careful caretakers of and try not to squander that gift. Again, as Cyril Connolly puts it, "The best thing that can happen for a writer is to be taken up very late or very early, when either old enough to take its measure, or so young that when dropped by society he has all life before him."[6]

Success breeds disillusionment as surely as does failure, and there are some temptations it's not easy to avoid.

Let me list a few.

First, the deep paralysis of repetition. If you've been rewarded for and accomplished at a certain kind of writing, it's hard to begin afresh; formula writers don't try to; indeed, it would shock their readership if the terms of engagement were changed. But many more serious artists play less to their weakness than strength, and sometimes this too can become formulaic: Think of the late Hemingway or Faulkner and the risks of repetition should come clear. The rhythms of the prose are constant, the syntax and character constructs and thematic concerns stay the same. But it's all habitual, a kind of shadowboxing enacted in slow motion; there's no creative challenge while they practice their old moves.

Nor is it always easy to find a new true subject. If what you're best at is, say, evoking the hallucinatory terrors of war, the likelihood you'll write persuasively about high school romance is slim; if you're fascinated by the interaction of members of a family, then your book about a hermit will likely fail to persuade. Any writer who's successful, young, will be so in part because of personal history and even, it may be, obsession; if there's an expectant audience established as a result of that obsession, the writer strays at risk. Sir Arthur Conan Doyle tried to kill off his creature Sherlock Holmes (in order to write something other than detective stories); a disappointed public, clamoring for further "adventures," forced Doyle to reverse himself and conjure up the return of Holmes.

A corollary here. Self-indulgence is hard to avoid, and particularly so when what you've done has been much rewarded; few friends or colleagues of the powerful will argue that a project had better be abandoned or a page be cut. There's a contract to sign and money to make or applause and a prize to receive; why should one cease producing what was praised before? This goes some distance, I think, to explaining the repetitive effusions of established authors when there's no one to simply say: *No.*

Second is the obverse of the first. For those writers who equate growth with change, the need to alter style and subject can itself be self-defeating. To write to your weakness and not to your strength is admirable, perhaps, but in its own way self-indulgent; it's why a realist might try her hand at surrealism, a fabulist write science fiction, and so on and so forth. Look at the melodramatic fantasy of Graham Greene's *Doctor Fischer of Geneva* and you'll see the risks not of consistency but willed experiment. At the end of their careers, John Cheever and Bernard Malamud did shift their ground, with mixed results; they simply weren't up to innovation and *Oh What a Paradise It Seems* or *The People* are gestures at a new mode, ill-advised.

Let me stress that these writers are ones I admire; they aren't easy targets or simple to dismiss. And perhaps it's an instance of damned if you do, damned if you don't; as the years and wealth accrete it's harder to evoke impoverished youth. So we get the unedifying spectacle of someone like James Baldwin living in pasha-like luxury in southern France and writing with decreased authority about Harlem's lean mean streets. Or Norman Mailer and Saul Bellow in their eighties writing as though on automatic pilot about the erotic high jinks and adventures of young men. Again I repeat that these are artists of great caliber and daring, great ambition and attainment; why they run down, run out of steam—beyond the merely biological aspect of depletion—is, I think, a complex question, and best answered case by case.

But this is not the place for detailed particular assessments; I'm not offering a series of critical biographies and, I hope, not an autobiography either. I still tell myself (as no doubt did those other authors) that the work I'm working on is the one that counts. Each morning when I sit to write I persuade myself, or try to, that the blank page to be blackened will be masterful by morning's end; this holds as true for the unpublished student as for Pulitzer Prize recipients in their honored age. It's that "willing suspension of disbelief"[7] which Coleridge stipulates as a necessary condition for a reader or member of an audience; in this case suspended disbelief is what the *writer* needs. It's the necessary *pre*condition, really, for all members of the guild—whether they be an apprentice, journeyman laborer, or master in the craft.

All writers recognize the difference, or should, between aspiration and achievement—between their dream of deathless prose and the piece of more or less iridescent mediocrity which they have just produced. All writers need believe the best work lies ahead. It's the kind of disease we call health to think that what we're about to create is splendid and not second rate; else how and why continue?

To know, I mean truly *know*—as might a basketball player or ballerina—that the best is behind you is to turn to drink or dithering or to an oven or gun. A few modest and decorous authors—think of E. M. Forster or Eudora Welty—withdraw into silence and declare at a certain point in their career, Enough's enough. But most of us go on and on, unable or unwilling to break a lifetime's habit of wrangling with language, and happy to be allowed, even encouraged, to do so. Most of us, when asked which book has been our favorite, will answer (hopefully, wishfully, truthfully), "The next."

• • •

In a celebrity culture, what matters is name recognition, and it might therefore seem that "lastingness" proves crucial in the arc of a career. Yet a specific aspect of the art scene favors youth. A new discovery is cost efficient to promote and requires less investment than the tried and true. Well-funded museums and dealers can acquire a Van Dyck or a Holbein, but if you plan to sponsor an artist it's smarter to do so while the "talent" is just starting out. In sheer financial terms it's hard to mount a gallery show or offer new work from "old masters"; these are rare and expensive to buy. So it's scarcely an accident that literary agents flock to creative writing programs or gallery owners visit studios in search of a beginner; the available Botticellis and Vermeers just aren't numerous enough, and most of their known paintings hang on institutional walls. When the "lost" Caravaggio was found some years ago in Dublin it made an enormous art-world splash, and no dealer of the present day could hope to have ten Gainsboroughs for sale.

This is less clearly the case for composers; the concert-going public tends to prefer recognizable programs from the near or distant past. But they're buying, of course, a performance, not the work of art itself; the investment here consists only of a ticket and an evening's time. Bach, Beethoven, and Brahms are surefire attractions, whereas three unknowns whose last names start with B might play an empty room. "Classical music" announces itself by the yoked adjective and noun; the two form a linked pair. It's the bane of present-day composers that the world of concert halls and orchestras remains so retrospective, and the tastes of its audience tradition-steeped; modern compositions have a hard time being aired.

In the popular music scene, however, the present erases the past. Last season's OK Go is this year's Plain White T's; next year's sensation may still be in school. The names of bands and début groups are dizzying in their prolixity and rapid shift. Taylor Swift, Kelly Clarkson, and Pink remain, as of this writing, hot; Jewel, Dido, and Madonna are lukewarm at best. How long Lady Gaga and Katy Perry will flourish is, in 2010, anyone's guess, but the Backstreet Boys and the Spice Girls are "so over." The economy of management here resembles that of the collector and art dealer; newer is cheaper and the chance of profit therefore greater. It's the next and not the last new sound that makes public noise.

These are issues of commerce, not talent, but the former and the latter intertwine. And one major implication for the less-than-superstar artist is how difficult it grows just to stay in play. The "midlist" writer is an endangered species; so are the painters and sculptors who fail to sell in galleries, the composers who don't get to hear their work performed. The early splash becomes a ripple in the soon-to-be-stilled pond. There are few fates as melancholy as that of an overweight crooner belting out the song that made his or her career some thirty years before; to continue regaling an audience with "Over the

Rainbow" or "American Pie" is to be caught in the time warp of early success. Innovation is at odds with repetition, and each artist must manage both. For a year or three or five the "overnight sensation" rides high on a wave, and then the crest flattens to trough.

• • •

Edward Said, in a collection of essays posthumously titled *On Late Style*,[8] argues that a certain kind of artist flourishes in contrariety. What Dylan Thomas urged as "rage, rage against the dying of the light" is, in Said's analysis, a central attribute of the work of Richard Strauss and Luchino Visconti and, in his last plays, William Shakespeare. (It's worth remembering, perhaps, that Thomas died at thirty-nine, and the villanelle "Do Not Go Gentle into That Good Night" was written to his father.) The critic's list includes Constantine Cavafy, Jean Genet, Glenn Gould, and in every case what he admires is oppositional intransigence. Not the ripeness or the readiness but the resistance is all.

Unsurprisingly, what engaged the dying Said's attention is these artists' refusal to accommodate to our somewhat easy formulation that with old age comes wisdom, the grace of resignation, the comforts of perspective, and so on and so forth. He doesn't quote, but might have, Yeats's fierce quatrain, "The Spur," which represents this stance:[9]

> You think it horrible that lust and rage
> Should dance attention upon my old age;
> They were not such a plague when I was young;
> What else have I to spur me into song?

David Galenson, in a recent book called *Old Masters and Young Geniuses*,[10] argues a different point. He draws a distinction between "experimental" artists—witness Leonardo or Cézanne, always dissatisfied with and constantly revising work—and "conceptual" ones—witness Raphael or Picasso, who made cartoons or studies for the compositions they then left unaltered. For the "experimental" artist there's a lifelong groping toward an unattainable ideal; for the latter "conceptual" group the important work will likely be conceived of and achieved whole cloth when young. Galenson is an economist and much of his book is devoted to graphs of what sells best and when, in the course of a career, it was produced. But he's on to something, I suspect, and for that group of ceaseless strivers (often miserable, always doubt-hounded as they search) the motto is Cézanne's: "I seek in painting."[11] Whereas Picasso announced, "I don't seek; I find."[12]

• • •

For the elderly practitioner, perseverance is, just as much as for the apprentice, a necessary component of the production of art. Continued health, sufficient comfort so that work is not an agony, continued expectation that what you write might be read. (If you're a composer, similarly, the hope is that your work be heard; if you're a painter or sculptor, that it will be seen.) And something else it's harder to define, that may perhaps be best described as the willingness to stay *interested,* to pay the kind of alert attention to the world around you that the wide-eyed young routinely pay.

I can remember when each morning seemed a burnished, shining thing, when every afternoon and night brought with it the possibility of something or someone not known before. Today there's very little new beneath the fictive sun. When I was a beginning writer everything was mill-grist, every conversation worth transcribing or embroidering, each encounter consequential and all emotion fresh. It happens, still, but rarely—that inner imperative: the voice that urges one to pay attention, to *learn.* More often there's exhaustion, a weary inability to persuade oneself that words matter or that an experience merits the recording; with so much verbiage everywhere, and so much of it fouled or wasted, why add your own daily extrusion to the language dump?

The novel is, by and large, a hopeful genre: full of brass and energy, with happy resolutions and virtue triumphant and vice defeated. Or if the mode is tragic and the ending sad, the novelist and his or her characters have waged a valiant struggle and lost a goodly fight. Inertia fails to power plots; even the novels of Samuel Beckett or books about mortality like *The Autumn of the Patriarch* by Gabriel García Márquez or *The Death of Artemio Cruz* by Carlos Fuentes are filled with remembered action and reenacted scenes. It's more often than not an exuberant form, a "baggy monster" high-stepping its way into flight.

But all of this gets harder and harder to manage with conviction. I was born in England, where "fiction" and "fable" edged up against the accusation "fib." "Don't tell a story," warned my childhood nanny, because even then I had the preprofessional inclination to improve upon flat fact. (Why walk through a field without monsters or a dungeon without dragons; why vanquish fifty enemies when five hundred might have appeared?) This impulse to embroider truth, to "tell a story," seems year by year more difficult to manage and childish to sustain. Even that enchanting preamble "Once upon a time" grows dull, and the postscript, "They lived happily ever after," is—not to put too fine a point on it—absurd. And yet a writer must believe that a tale's invented incidents and made-up characters are worth describing, worth the damning or the saving. So the failure of illusion is perhaps the most insidious of those enemies of promise I've attempted here to list: Disbelief gets harder to suspend.

In other art forms, this seems somehow less an

issue; we've come to understand that Monet at Giverny, painting water lilies for his private pleasure, broke new artistic ground. He sold few of them during his lifetime; they're his most coveted canvases now.[13] Think of the elderly Rembrandt consigned to his studio and self-portraiture, or the old deaf Goya and his black bleak paintings; they're what we most value today. (This is a different model from, for example, those of Schubert and Mozart or Kafka and Keats or Caravaggio and Van Gogh: artists cut off in their early prime while unable to garner commissions or to sell their work—dead young and ill and self-tormented and poor. By contrast these older artists each had known considerable success; in their final years they renounced it.) They could presumably have gone on producing portraits of dukes and ladies and self-satisfied burghers and been well compensated for their pains; something compelled them to set out anew. Beethoven's late quartets follow a similar pattern, and Stradivari was past sixty when he changed the template of the cello; he produced fine violins well into his nineties. It can, I mean, be done.

Not often, however, and why not, I wonder, and that's the real mystery of lastingness—what happens during one's lifetime, not somehow after the fact. They say sixty is the new forty, seventy the new fifty in physical terms; perhaps it's not too much to hope that energy too might be retained for the difficult work of invention, that dream dreamed at a desk. In older age such dreaming can become a kind of nightmare, while habit fades to mere repetition, repetition to what James called, in his euphemism for death, the "distinguished thing." There *is* a kind of death-in-life where imagination's engine slips its gears and stalls—or, to shift the metaphor, where the big-bellied sail of invention luffs until becalmed. Or where we tack to change our course but gain no actual ground.

In ancient Greece the paired perils facing the traveler—monstrous rocks and whirlpools—were known as Scylla and Charybdis. It's thought that these twin killers lay off the coast of Sicily, where Odysseus was able, with the help of the Goddess Athena, to squeeze through. It took both skill and luck to navigate between them: to avoid being swallowed by the sea or dashed against the cliffs. The name of the shipwrecked is legion, their number beyond counting, yet every once in a great while a storied hero manages to sail between the dangers safely, and the song gets sung.

• • •

At the start of this inquiry, therefore, here are a few first assertions:

To stay alive and stay awake are not always one and the same.

The work imagined is not the work achieved.

Youth may be wasted on the young, but age may just as often be wasted on the elderly.

Every engagement does not result in marriage; not every marriage lasts. I speak here of the union between artists and their art.

The "genius" dead before his or her time is a romantic construct; realism argues that when we're done we're done.

Some things continue; some don't.

What might have been is therefore an irrelevance: Thomas Chatterton at sixty, Sylvia Plath happily domestic, Hemingway or Faulkner sober—none of these pertain.

The long view and the near are linked; bifocals help.

All young artists have been "promising." Some deliver on that promise and become "distinguished." The trick is to negotiate the forty or the fifty intervening years.

Rarely—very rarely, and yet it still can happen—the final act improves upon the first.

CHAPTER TWO

Mere Oblivion

. . . Last scene of all,
That ends this strange eventful history,
Is second childishness and mere oblivion,
Sans teeth, sans eyes, sans taste, sans every thing

William Shakespeare
As You Like It, II, vii

Eubie Blake, the ragtime pianist, was one hundred years old when he died.[1] Blake stayed quick-witted, nimble tongued—and nimble fingered in his music-making—till the very end. At his centenary celebration, the pioneer of boogie-woogie said, "If I'd known I was gonna live this long, I'd have taken better care of myself."

Grandma Moses did take care, dying at one hundred one. Her family still runs a vegetable stand in the upstate village of Eagle Bridge, New York, and the landscape she reported on looks much the same. Photographs and video clips of the spry, white-haired old lady suggest she loved the role she played: America's bespectacled witness, painstakingly outlining hayfields and snowfields and horses and barns and fruit trees and, from household chimneys, smoke. Self-taught and wholly familiar with the world she memorialized, "Grandma" appeared to take late fame in stride; journalists would seek her out, not the other way around.

Many great artists lived long. We know that Titian (Tiziano Vecellio) died in the city of Venice on August 27, 1576, having been for sixty years the undisputed master of the Venetian School. Although a large proportion of his thousand canvases were worked on by assistants, he remains among the most prolific and accomplished painters of all time. His color sense was sumptuous, his compositions unerring, and his fleshly nudes and "Titian-haired" beauties still appear to breathe. The portrait of Pietro Aretino hanging in the Frick Collection is a masterpiece of psychological acuteness; shave the man and change his clothes and he could be paying a visit to that museum today. Titian claimed to have been born in 1477, which would make him ninety-nine;

birth records of the period are inexact, however, and he may have been a stripling who died at ninety-five.

Nonagenarians are frequent in the history of art. An incomplete sampling would include the Italian painter Giorgio di Chirico, and the Greek dramatist Sophocles, who wrote *Oedipus at Colonus* near the end of his very long life. According to a probably inexact tradition, Sophocles demonstrated competence—disproving his son's accusation that he had grown feeble-minded—by reciting entire speeches from the "Colonus" while a rapt audience wept.

Louise Bourgeois at ninety-six enjoyed a retrospective in 2008 at New York's Guggenheim Museum. Carmen Herrera—who sold her first painting at the age of eighty-nine—was described in a 2009 *New York Times* front-page story as "At 94, the Hot New Thing."[2] Pablo Casals was ninety-six at the time of his death, Georgia O'Keeffe ninety-eight. At the age of ninety-one Somerset Maugham expired, as did Jean Sibelius and Pablo Picasso; Knut Hamsun lived till ninety-two. A. E. Housman "gave up the ghost" at ninety-three, as did P. G. Wodehouse and Oskar Kokoschka. George Bernard Shaw survived till ninety-four, and Marc Chagall ninety-seven.

Mere octogenarians include the painters Francesco Guardi and Lucas Cranach the Elder, the writers Victor

Hugo and William Wordsworth, and the sculptor Dona-tello. Those who lived till eighty-one include the artists Constantin Brancusi, Georges Braque, Johann Wolfgang von Goethe, Walter Sickert, and George Stubbs. Lev Tolstoy and Francisco Goya died at eighty-two. Edgar Degas persisted till the age of eighty-three, and Henri Matisse eighty-four; so too did Sean O'Casey and Max Ernst. To take a further sampling, Giovanni Bellini, Michelangelo Buonarroti, Frans Hals, Thomas Hardy, Hermann Hesse, Jean-Auguste-Dominique Ingres, Arthur Miller, Claude Monet, Ezra Pound, Georges Rouault, Harriet Beecher Stowe, Richard Strauss, Igor Stravinsky, Giuseppe Verdi, and Ralph Vaughan Wil-liams all lived to their late eighties, and Hokusai—the self-described "old man mad about painting"—died when eighty-nine, in 1849.

As Henry Wadsworth Longfellow points out in his *Morituri Salutamos:* "Cato learned Greek at eighty; Sophocles / Wrote his grand *Oedipus,* and Simonides / Bore off the prize for verse from his compeers, / When each had numbered more than fourscore years." This is a writer writing about writers, but there are other occu-pations particularly congenial-seeming to the elderly, and in which they flourish. The architect Christopher Wren died when he was ninety, and Alvar Aalto, Walter Gropius, Ludwig Mies van der Rohe, and Frank Lloyd Wright all approached that age. Architects require time to rise through the ranks of an office, or to establish their own; they rarely receive important commissions till fifty or sixty years old. Marcel Breuer, Le Corbusier, and Louis Kahn—to name only a few practitioners— were at work and productive in their final years. Most present "stars" of the architectural firmament—Norman Foster, Frank Gehry, Richard Meier, Rafael Moneo, I. M. Pei, Renzo Piano, and Richard Rogers among them—have reached "a certain age."

Another such profession is that of conductor. The aerobic exercise of conducting from a podium is self-evidently beneficial, and elderly orchestra leaders seem everywhere engaged. Men like Thomas Beecham, Adrian Boult, Arthur Fiedler, Otto Klemperer, Pierre Monteux, Georg Solti, and Arturo Toscanini performed well into their seventies and eighties; Leopold Stokowski died at ninety-five. There are of course precocious conductors and visionary architects who compel admiration when young, but the generality would seem to hold: It helps to be "mature." These occupations, however, depend on a community and rely on the collective; they cannot be pursued alone and fall outside the confines of my study. As suggested in the Introduction, my focus is on the individual in three "solo" creative fields: literature, music, and the visual arts.

Artists in their seventies are legion. The briefest of lists might include (I group them not alphabetically or by medium but by their age at death): Hans Christian Andersen, Canaletto, Benvenuto Cellini, Honoré Daumier (70); Daniel Defoe, Piet Mondrian, Nicolas Poussin, Maurice Utrillo, Tennessee Williams (71); Barbara Hepworth, Henry James, Algernon Charles Swinburne, Walt Whitman (72); Noel Coward, Antoni Gaudi, El Greco, William Butler Yeats (73); Jean-Honoré Fragonard, George Frederick Handel, Fernand Léger, Tiepolo, Mark Twain (74); Raoul Dufy, Samuel Johnson, Andrea Mantegna, Jacopo Tintoretto, (75); Edward Elgar, T. S. Eliot, Joseph Turner (76); Edith Sitwell, Jules Verne (77); Alexander Calder, Jean-Baptiste Camille Corot, Euripides, Henrik Ibsen, Vladimir Nabokov, Paolo Uccello (78); and Pierre Bonnard and Edgar Varèse, who lived until seventy-nine. What the French have called the *troisième age*—that third category beyond childhood and maturity—now extends indefinitely; a fourth or *quatrième age* may prove necessary soon.

• • •

All this raises the question of actuarial tables and life expectancy as such.[3] During the Roman Empire and in the "Pax Romana," the average life span of the citizen is thought to have been twenty-eight; today, in the "Pax Americana," the average citizen expects fifty additional years. As recently as 1900, the average life expectancy was a mere forty-five. And, as those who deal with Medicare and Medicaid and the Social Security Administration more and more urgently remind us, the fastest-growing segment of the American population is the elderly. Our aging populace constitutes a major shift of emphasis within the "body politic," and its effects are just beginning to come clear.

One need be neither a scientist, sociologist, nor politician to understand that changes must be made in our treatment of "senior citizens"; medical, fiscal, housing, retirement, and transportation policies all need to be adjusted as the nation's men and women grow older month by year. Teleologically speaking, and if we count back from the end point, it's almost as though we no longer need die; we gain in life expectancy for every year we live. It's a version of Xeno's paradox: We halve the distance to our "goal" yet never quite attain it—or only when the complex system of the body at length stops functioning. Too, a disproportionate amount of our medical costs and expenditures are incurred in the final six months.

These are not merely American problems. Countries as diverse as Finland and San Marino face the same issues acutely—and the longer-lived their populace the more urgent the problems become. The population of the planet is growing exponentially in part because of longer life: Pandemics are averted or controlled, childbearing years extend, and we do not die as rapidly once ill. When William Butler Yeats observed "That is no country for old men," he was referring to an Ireland that had become—comparatively speaking—comfortable, and where the old lived well.

Instead it's the youthful population that remains, worldwide, at risk. The infant mortality rate is a major factor in any statistical survey of how long we live. Indeed, it's the principal marker—whether we're discussing societies of 20,000, 2000, or 200 years ago. War, malnutrition, starvation, and the failure to inoculate against disease all take their lethal toll. Many of the countries with the lowest life expectancies (such as Botswana, Central African Republic, Guinea-Bissau, Lesotho, Malawi, Mozambique, Namibia, South Africa, Zambia, and Zimbabwe) suffer from very high rates of HIV/AIDS infection, with adult prevalence rates ranging from 10 to 38 percent. Those who inhabit Swaziland will live an average of 32.23 years. Almost without exception, the men and women who contract HIV/AIDS in these impoverished nations will rapidly succumb.

For them, the Hobbesian description of life as "nasty, brutish and short" holds all too true. (Thomas Hobbes wrote *Leviathan* while in his sixties and lived till ninety-one.) Sex traffic, gang warfare, and child slavery each constitute a human scourge that also impacts age. The danger of conscription or forced manual labor—life in the army or the mines—further reduces the life span of those whom Frantz Fanon called "the wretched of the earth." I don't mean by this (it's neither statistically nor medically accurate) that human beings in old age are less susceptible to mortal shocks than men and women in life's prime, but only that they have the habit of survival and have escaped youth's risks.

For by whatever measure and plotted on whichever graph, it's clear we're getting older, and one crucial aspect of "lastingness" is how well we do so. According to *The World Factbook* for 2007, worldwide average life expectancy is now 65.86 years—men can expect to live to 63.89 and women an average 67.84 years. The longest-lived nationals inhabit Andorra, with a life span of 83.52 years; they are followed by the citizens of Macau at 82.27 and Japan at 82.02. The United States, for all its vaunted prosperity and medical expertise, ranks forty-fifth worldwide, with an average life expectancy hovering between the ages of 77 and 78. Its impoverished neighbor, Cuba, after decades of embargo, has a population that can expect the same.

Retirement communities may be a boon to real estate developers, and the well-heeled use motorized wheelchairs, but the poor in urban and rural America still suffer from very high rates of pre-term birth and infant mortality (which constitutes the reason we rank number forty-five). And youth itself means something new; we're far more precocious as well as later-starting than would have been the case two hundred years ago. We're both more independent and dependent than was the rule in previous times, both more connected to the world and protected from it. A cell phone permits us to travel yet stay in touch with home. A credit card enables both purchasing power and debt. The paradox attaching to our nation's young is everywhere made manifest; childbearing gets deferred by those who marry late or embark on careers—and when these ·no-longer-quite-so-fertile couples require fertility treatments, quadruplets may result.

My interest here, however, is what happens in old age. We keep our teeth longer, our backs are less bent. Central heat, indoor plumbing, and air conditioning have changed the expectations attaching to hygiene and therefore health. X-rays and antibiotics have materially improved our physical condition; Viagra and Cialis and an arsenal of face creams promise perpetual youth. And, as TV ads for pharmaceuticals constantly remind us, "You're only as old as you feel."

Yet if you study photographs of soldiers in the Civil War or look at those who stand on breadlines in the Great Depression, you'll see a different national profile than that of our nation today. Our waistlines have enlarged. We drive and fly great distances but rarely walk more than five miles. Jackie Gleason's sitcom character in the 1950s—the heavyset, big-bellied Ralph

Kramden—would seem a svelte performer on television now. The epidemic of obesity that threatens to make our generation the first to live less long than its parents is a new phenomenon, engendered by "junk" food and insufficient exercise. "Assisted Living" compounds and "Home Health-Care Givers" are new phenomena also, and will almost surely increase.

These observations belabor the obvious, but "life expectancy" itself is coming into question as a useful measure, and all the more so if the organism's existence is artificially sustained. Some gerontologists suggest we consider instead such terms as "disability-free years" and the idea, at the end, of "compressed morbidity"; "health years" and "health span" have been recently proposed as substitutes for the all-inclusive statistical figure of "life years" or "life span." It's possible (consider the case of Terri Schiavo) to live for decades in a near vegetal state.

Is thirty thirty, forty forty? I mean by this that the meaning of such numbers may itself have changed. Anthropologists and archaeologists and paleontologists and forensic experts have accumulated evidence of bone and body mass in the young or elderly in previous times; we have some understanding of what it entailed to enter into combat in Thermopylae or Carthage or in the Ninth Crusade. We know about lead poisoning and cal-cification in hips. But it's impossible to truly know—to inhabit, as it were—the bodies of the ancient dead and feel what they were feeling when they made their morning oblation or drank their cup of wine. It's natural enough for us to imagine that Achilles and a contemporary actor or Helen of Troy and a modern movie star are similar of stature—that the hair and legs and breasts and waistlines of our famous ancestors look more or less equivalent in those who portray them today. But a visit to the Catacombs or a Hall of Armor dispels that illusion in terms of *size;* we're larger as a species and will no doubt continue to grow. If our breadth and bones have altered, if matters of shelter and nutrition transform the way we sleep and defecate, why would it not be also true that our ways of feeling young and old have changed?

Jane Austen, Honoré de Balzac, Miguel de Cervantes, Fyodor Dostoyevsky, George Eliot, Gustave Flaubert, and writers with surnames starting with the letters "G" through "Z" all attained maturity but not the age of seventy; must they therefore be excluded from our list? Is it possible that Mendelssohn, Mozart, Schubert, and the rest had used up their allotted span and did not in fact die young? When Shakespeare retired to Stratford-upon-Avon—having been born in that village in April 1564 and fated to die there in April 1616—was he a very old man?

• • •

William Shakespeare can't provide a true case study of "lastingness," since his is a case apart. The dimensions of his genius make him nonrepresentative; he was and is one of a kind. Perhaps no one in history—and certainly not in the English language—has reported on a greater range of characters and social class; from gardener to bishop, from fool to king, and "rude mechanical" to courtier he moved with almost insouciant ease and a dramatist's all-seeing eye. His "I" is multitudes.

What this means in theatrical terms is that he could shape-shift at "will." As Keats observed, the dramatist was supremely possessed of the faculty of "Negative Capability": the ability to enter a consciousness other than his own. Always, Shakespeare was able to argue both sides of a single question, inhabit warring adversaries, and phrase opposing views. This is a sine qua non of the theater, where men and women up on stage aren't stand-ins for their author but motivated characters with conflicting needs. And it's therefore doubly hard to say, *This* he endorses, *that* he rejects, *these* are his opinions and they do not change.

Take three of his great plays about love: *Romeo and Juliet*, and *Antony and Cleopatra*, and *The Winter's Tale*. They represent a progression from adolescent to middle-aged passion and then to enduring devotion (as in Hermione's sixteen years of faithfulness to the husband who had banished her). *Othello* and *Twelfth Night* and *Troilus and Cressida* and *A Midsummer Night's Dream* also are importantly concerned with romance and its entanglements. But do they mirror the mind of their creator, his own erotic infatuations, or are they simply charts of love's terrain? Are any of the antics so brilliantly portrayed onstage in some way self-reflexive? It's clear when he wrote them and clear in which order, but not so simple to interpret them in terms of autobiography. Did he consider suicide as does Romeo or find himself spellbound as was Antony or jealous as Leontes? Did he lust for ass-eared Bottom as does Queen Titania; was he seduced by someone's look-alike or enamored of cross-dressing twins? Does he endorse or disagree with his creature's famed pronouncement as to romantic behavior (in *A Midsummer Night's Dream*, act 3, scene 2): "Lord, what fools these mortals be!"[4]

We cannot know. We have too little evidence of Shakespeare's personal history to speculate with profit on his transition from youth to age and how or what he learned. To try—in the modern manner—to establish a connection between personal experience and articulated art is to be baffled throughout. We think he played the part of "old Adam" in *As You Like It* and possibly Oliver Martext. But did his son Hamnet's death importantly inflect his portrait of Prince Hamlet, and did he suffer depression while writing *Measure for Measure* or *King Lear*? Is *Troilus* the record of nervous collapse and does *Titus Andronicus* suggest he took pleasure in pain? Do *The Merry Wives of Windsor* and *All's Well That Ends Well* mean his sunny disposition was slated to prevail?

The answers are uncertain, and the only certainty is

that we cannot tell. We have documentary proof of birth and weddings, death and lawsuits, and within the welter of the texts reside a few fixed notions. There's the probably unhappy marriage to a woman some years his senior, the probably authentic devotion to a man some years his junior, the probably sincere conviction that daughters should obey their fathers and the probably personal dislike of dogs. All else is open to revision or, as Matthew Arnold put it, "Others abide our question. Thou art free."

Still, it's possible by reading him to come to a kind of consensus opinion on his thoughts about mortality and what age entails. And, since no one ever wrote about the human condition more tellingly, it seems appropriate to borrow from his language and use his expertise here. When proud King Lear declares himself "an old, fond, foolish man" and repeats his despairing "Never, never, never..." because his child will "come no more" we hear the voice of bitter wisdom and see a searing portrait of man at the end of his days. Near the very end, in fact, in *The Two Noble Kinsmen* (which he most likely co-wrote with John Fletcher in 1613–1614), Shakespeare describes an ancient grotesque in terms that one can only hope are not those of self-portraiture:

> The aged cramp
> Had screwed his square foot round,
> That gout had knit his fingers into knots,

Torturing convulsions from his globy eyes
Had almost drawn their spheres, that what was life
In him seemed torture.

(V, ii, l. 42–47)

From Macbeth's "the sere, the yellow leaf…" to Prospero's announcement that "Every third thought shall be my grave," the Swan of Avon seems to have been haunted by the prospect and then actuality of death. And long before "Tomorrow and tomorrow and tomorrow" engaged the bard's attention, he understood the stages of incremental age. Some of this is formulaic, a matter of convention, but the elderly were with him from the start. His assertion that "Old men forget" (*Henry V*), his evocation of John of Gaunt in *Richard II* and his description of "second childishness" as the final act of seven (*As You Like It*) all have the ring of witnessed truth and not mere rhetoric.

For life is a "brief candle," and soon to gutter out. When young Harry Percy dies (having been bested in single combat by Prince Hal) in *Henry IV, I*, he says gaspingly—there's only one word of these twenty-three that's more than monosyllabic:

But thoughts, the slaves of life, and life, time's fool,
And time, that takes survey of all the world,
Must have a stop….

(V, iv, l. 81–83)

"The fools of time" are everywhere in Shakespeare, and "the whirligig of time" must "bring in its revenges." He possesses the stoic's conviction that "death, a necessary end, will come when it will come"—or phrases this conviction through characters such as the soon-to-be-assassinated Julius Caesar. When her husband tells Calpurnia, "Of all the wonders that I yet have heard, it seems to me most strange that men should fear," he offers a reproof to those who would prolong their life expectancy by caution. When Prince Hamlet tells Horatio there's "a special providence in the fall of a sparrow" and urges acquiescence, he's saying, in effect, there's no gainsaying death. "The readiness is all," for Hamlet, although he has temporized much. The "divinity that shapes our ends / rough-hew them how we will" suggests both a willed submission to fate, and the farmer's skilled ability to finish off a hedge.

Think of that hedge as the form of a play, with its shaped duration. The hours and acts of theatrical time encompass decades often—particularly so in the Romances, where the logic of chronology gives way to a synoptic rendering of years. If in the comedies and history plays and tragedies Shakespeare busied himself with coherence—striving to make sense of things, stressing causal connections and linked tales—the late plays are less sequence bound or yoked to plausibility. It's as though the peerless artificer has had enough of artifice and now simply wants to tell stories (moving closer to the strategies of fiction than of verse). The masques and dumb-shows honor entertainment, and if a character gets pursued by a bear, why that's just part of the spectacle; the playwright had spent years competing with the bear-baiting rink next door.

Still, there's a growing impatience. The Romances echo the rhyming assertion in *Cymbeline* that—soon or late, no matter how we attempt to deny it—"golden lads and girls all must / as chimney sweepers, come to dust." One has the sense, in *The Tempest*, of incremental exhaustion, an old magician's readiness to quit the stage. That "our revels now are ended" comes almost as relief. When Caliban reminds his master, "You taught me language, and my profit on't / is I know how to curse," there's more than mere humor involved; such language is a burdensome gift, and one that its possessor seems willing to renounce.

Before this, of course, comes sweet music. If in *Cymbeline* we're told to "Fear no more the heat of the sun," during Ariel's song in *The Tempest* we're invited to imagine an almost alchemical shift:

> Full fathom five thy father lies.
> Of his bones are coral made;
> Those are pearls that were his eyes;
> Nothing of him that doth fade

> But doth suffer a sea-change
> Into something rich and strange.
>
> (1, ii, 400–405)

This "something rich and strange," as many critics have observed, has to do with necromancy, and takes as its near antecedent the transformation of Hermione from stone to flesh in the final sequence of *The Winter's Tale*. Both shifts are quasi-magical, with the playwright as the mage; the "sea-change" from living to lasting has to do with what endures when flesh "doth fade." And in such a reading, possibly, the fools of time are jesters at least as much as dupes; it's Feste and Lear's fool who most completely understand the way the cold wind blowing may turn to perfumed air—as well as the reverse. So when Prospero describes his own "most potent art" and declares himself prepared to abjure it, he nonetheless has mustered "cloud-capp'd towers" and "the great globe itself"—all conjured into language while the pageant fades. The playwright, ready to retire, must have known (in the very act of announcing he'd leave "not a rack behind") that the play would last.

In the sonnets in particular, Shakespeare considers what endures—even with an adleaven of braggadocio in such couplets as: "If this be error, and upon me proved / I never writ, nor no man ever loved." The dramas have few such referents to the act of composition; they were intended for performance and not as words on a page. When Malvolio pens a letter or Osric carries written instructions, the business of writing is stage business, and often as not those who rely on pen and paper are made fun of or made to seem inept.

Indeed, since his "scripts" antedate copyright protection, there was a kind of premium on *not* being published. Text was a closely kept secret. John Heminges and Henry Condell, fellow members of his acting troupe, made a profit out of Shakespeare's writing only when he no longer produced it, and the first Folio appeared seven years after his death. The company of the King's Men did not want their language available for performance by their rivals in the provinces; the fair copy of a play existed more as a prompter's script than speeches intended for strangers to read. The actors had their individual parts pasted into strips or rolls, not a full version of the text to carry home and memorize and then, perhaps, dispose of for a fee. Our practical man of the theater from Stratford would no doubt be amazed to know how widely his dramas are published and studied in silence today.

But this is not the case with poetry, which by the sixteenth century had a long-standing tradition as written artifact. When Shakespeare penned his sonnets, he did so in the expectation that they would be preserved. The page is much referenced here. As suggested above (and in contradistinction to the plays) the poems are full of allusions to their own written existence, and they stake claims on "lastingness" almost habitually. The theme of immortality in verse was a conventional one, much practiced by his predecessors; the ravages of time and mutability and their effects on youthful beauty had been established as a subject before the sonnet form.

The final written word is, often, proudly predictive, as in the declaration with which Sonnet 18 ends:

> But thy eternal summer shall not fade,
> Nor lose possession of that fair thou ow'st,
> Nor shall Death brag thou wand'rest in his shade,
> When in eternal lines to time thou grow'st.
> So long as men can breathe or eyes can see,
> So long lives this, and this gives life to thee.

There's a near boastfulness in the future-facing certainty that his craft will live as long as "eyes can see," a trumpeting that puts death in its place. The "eternal lines" are Shakespeare's own, and the object of his praise can claim "eternal summer" though the season itself—as in line four of that sonnet—"hath all too short a date." The poem begins, of course, with the rhetorical question "Shall I compare thee to a summer's day?" and the implicit answer is, Why bother? since art's delight persists.

Too, these poems "hold the mirror up to nature" and describe what will not last. Shakespeare was always precocious; he had a quicker ratio to the passage of time than ordinary men. And when he wrote the following, he would have been barely thirty. No recognition of old age, no description of youth's fleetingness is more incisive than his:

Sonnet 73

That time of year thou mayst in me behold
When yellow leaves, or none, or few do hang
Upon those boughs which shake against the cold,
Bare ruin'd choirs where late the sweet birds sang.
In me thou seest the twilight of such day
As after sunset fadeth in the west,
Which by and by black night doth take away,
Death's second self, that seals up all in rest.
In me thou seest the glowing of such fire
That on the ashes of his youth doth lie,
As the death-bed whereon it must expire,
Consum'd with that which it was nourish'd by.
   This thou perceivs't, which makes thy love more strong
   To love that well, which thou must leave ere long.

We do know he moved to the country, with only a few trips to London in the final years. He bought New Place, one of the principal dwellings in Stratford-upon-

Avon, as early as 1597. Shakespeare's father had been prosperous there before his fortunes altered, and Anne Hathaway's family came from solid local stock. But the playwright earned real money in his chosen trade, and he seems to have known he would spend it at home; for years he made long-distance purchases, both large and small, of land. "In May 1602 and again in July 1605 Shakespeare made very substantial investments in 'yard-lands' and leases of tithes in the Stratford area. He was now, in addition to a successful playwright and actor, a significant local rentier and one of Stratford's leading citizens."[5] While in London he lived modestly, in rented rooms; once back in the place of his birth he planned to make a show.

The Tempest, with its grand renunciation scene, has long been read as a kind of retirement party the play-wright threw for himself. Prospero, who can do almost anything, does next to nothing in punishment of the rivals by whom he has been wronged. Instead, he mounts a fete, proclaiming, "The rarer action is in virtue than in vengeance." Then, having done well by his daughter, Miranda (as would Shakespeare by his beloved daughter Susanna), the duke withdraws to meditation and "every third thought" of the grave. So when he asks for audience indulgence, in the play's final moment, he's asking for more than applause; like Caliban and Ariel he hopes to be released. Though we have little information on his physical condition, it's likely the writer expected a longer life of retirement than the one he lived; he was buried, according to the Stratford register, on April 25, 1616, at the age of fifty-two.

It was a quiet passing: sudden, unremarked, and according to one account brought on by a drinking bout with his old cronies Michael Drayton and Ben Jonson. But there's no real record of excess, and not many die of a night in a bar—as did young Christopher Marlowe in a tavern brawl. We don't really know what killed Shakespeare, whether he suffered a wasting disease or caught a sudden chill. What's clear is he had *wanted* to retire from the theater and was not forced to do so, and also that his planned withdrawal was not absolute. Stratford was to be his principal but not sole residence; by analogy he now might be a retired chief executive of the company of the King's Men who remains on a retainer or serves as a consultant.

From time to time he lent a hand to his handpicked successor, John Fletcher (witness his work on *The Two Noble Kinsmen*), and he did purchase a place in Blackfriars as, plausibly, a *pied-à-terre* as well as a London investment. The best guess is he'd had enough of the hurly-burly of daily production and wanted, as it were, to leave "the cloud-capped towers, the gorgeous palaces, the solemn temples, the great globe itself...behind." He was tired; he'd worked long and hard.

Yet the charms of domesticity were never compelling to Shakespeare, and he famously left his wife only his "second-best bed." His daughter Judith married a man of whom he disapproved, and to whom he left nothing by name. He did make several small bequests—his sword to Thomas Combe; money to buy "rings" for his old colleagues Heminges, Condell, and Richard Burbage; five pounds to Thomas Russell—then gave the bulk of the estate to Susanna (whose husband, John Arden, was a man he trusted). Shakespeare's last will and testament was conceived of in January 1616 and signed by him in a shaky hand on March 25. That he died at New Place some twenty days later suggests he knew he wasn't well and wanted to put things in order.

The poetry and plays were of unequaled quality; he no doubt knew that too. To play at word games as did he, they were Will's true testament, and had been built to last. But the whole idea of "lastingness" would have been a little different in the Elizabethan period, or in Jacobean England. The great lost works of Greece and Rome had recently been found again, the great words of the Bible were being newly minted in the King James version. We've come, as a civilization, to value that which went before and to preserve it zealously; in the expansive Renaissance—of which Shakespeare was principal spokesman—what mattered was forward-facing discovery and not retrospect.

This is debatable, of course. Yet no one who wrote in English ever invented more of it, and neologism is in its very essence a strategy of innovation; it pays the past scant heed. "What's past is prologue," as he wrote, and even the history plays would have provided his audience with newfound information; the Plantagenet and Tudor kings that Shakespeare brought to life onstage are familiar to us now *because* he imagined them then.

Further, one can argue that the playwright's use of source material is in its nature piratical; the past was there for plundering, the histories and chronicles available for alteration like the New Place he newly tricked out. He was "disrespectful" of Plutarch and Holinshed and others, and it seems fair to say he would have expected equivalent treatment from those who might adapt him in their turn. Now we are scrupulous to a fault, particular and scholarly to the best of our cautious discernment, but Thomas Bowdler, who censored him, or those who let Cordelia and Lear enjoy a happy ending are in some sense faithful to the playwright's revisionist spirit.

In *Becoming Shakespeare: The Unlikely Afterlife That Turned a Provincial Playwright into the Bard,*[6] Jack Lynch convincingly argues that our response to Shakespeare was not foreordained. A series of events ensued, a series of sponsors emerged, and the collective efforts of later generations were necessary before a retired playwright and theater manager became the "Immortal Bard." This takes nothing away from his greatness but may put it in perspective; at the end of his career he knew little of the currency his work enjoys today.

So it would seem unlikely he spent his last years worrying about the future fate of *Coriolanus* or *Two Gentlemen of Verona*—a self-appointed archivist of the self-engendered canon. More likely that he supervised his gardens than his texts. And as suggested at this chapter's start, what a seventeenth-century man in his fifties might have been feeling in physical terms is open to conjecture. He may have felt both old and weak while he wrote *The Tempest*, or may instead have reveled in possession of his gift. As Sonnet 91 suggests, "Some glory in their birth, some in their skill / Some in their wealth, some in their body's force...." We know little of the process but are graced with the result. However personal the portrait of that aging necromancer, however much a self-portrait we think it today to have been at the time, Prospero's spectacle-making would prove as "swan song" to have been Shakespeare's finale.

But when—as in Jaques's soliloquy—the "last scene of all" would end "this strange eventful history" it would not arrive as "mere oblivion." For here is our preeminent example both of "lastingness" and its discussion; Shakespeare's gallery of characters includes both those who die onstage and those who live to render them immortal. Continually he tries—as Hamlet urges Horatio—to "tell my story right."

• • •

To *tell my story right* is a demanding challenge; Horatio describes himself as "more an antique Roman than a Dane." He would have preferred to fall on his sword, not serve as wordy witness to his companion's actions or be the spokesman charged with after-the-fact explanation. William Shakespeare, dead at fifty-two, drew the template for but did not himself survive to great old age.

Increasingly, we do. In the ensuing pages, I discuss elderly artists—in survey mode in Chapter Three, three at a time in Chapters Four through Six. The rule (Giuseppi di Lampedusa stands as the exception that proves it) is that these men and women lived and worked till seventy or older. The figures hereafter profiled each knew "the sere, the yellow leaf"—more prevalent these centuries than during the Elizabethan era—and wrote or painted or made music till the end. How did their art enlarge or shift; *did* their art enlarge or shift; and what may we learn?

CHAPTER THREE

Brief Long Lives

The mother of the Muses, we are taught,
Is Memory: she has left me; they remain,
And shake my shoulder, urging me to sing
About the summer days, my loves of old.
Alas! alas! is all I can reply.
>> Walter Savage Landor, "Memory"

A s the previous chapter suggests, many artists have lived long. The work of old age has no fixed prescription, no one way of being accomplished. For every nonagenarian who drinks only fruit juice and does yoga daily, there's another with a glass of wine or puffing a cigar. "The art of losing," as Elizabeth Bishop so piercingly wrote, "isn't hard to master." But winning too—or, at any rate, remaining in the game—entails a kind of mastery. And sometimes the two are coeval: To continue is to succeed.

Walter Savage Landor, nearing ninety, wrote his poem "Memory," a searing meditation on the loss of what he'd loved. Leoš Janáček, by contrast, grew enamored of a woman almost forty years his junior and composed the great late string quartets. Landor and Janáček, it could be argued, did their best work last. To release from its confines the slackening ego is possible in older age, and it may prove fruitful. So too can the opposite impulse: an embrace of the transient and fleet. For every voyager inspired by travel, another yearns for home; for every artist who begins anew, another dreams of constancy, and there's no single behavioral model to which they all subscribe.

Still, while walking in the forest, we like to identify trees. Thumbnail sketches follow (in alphabetical not chronological order) for nine men and women from the near and somewhat distant past.

• • •

Thomas Hardy (1840–1928) is an enigmatic figure and not simple to assess. Born poor, he died rich; a melancholy and secretive man, he was happy in the Savile Club and pleased to be invited to the tables of the great. A country boy who spent—as soon as he could afford it—the season in London, Hardy was bookish but self-taught; although (and possibly because) he never went to college, he gloried in the offer of honorary degrees. Most successful as a novelist, he gave up the writing of novels when "only" fifty-five; *Jude the Obscure,* his last major work of fiction, excoriated the society he had been at pains to join. His writing veered wildly from care-filled to care-less; few authors have published so much that is splendid adjacent to so much that's bad.

The son of a builder and trained as an architect, he designed his own house, Max Gate, but paid more attention to the walls and trees than electricity or indoor plumbing, of which there was next to none. "He slept in an unheated bedroom and had his hot water brought up in jugs."[1] A prodigious walker, he learned to ride a bicycle and enjoyed several sojourns in Europe, but Dorset remained his true home. His ill-tempered terrier—named after his fictional Wessex—received the kind of lavish affection the writer elsewhere withheld. A devoted son and sibling, he had no children of his own; family quarrels were frequent, and his first marriage foundered as his fame increased. The admiring consort of Hardy's old age, Florence, described her predecessor, Emma, as insane. His conflicted heart was cut out of his body and buried in his first wife's grave in the churchyard at Stinsford in Dorset, where Hardy's parents and grandparents also lay; the cremated rest of him was interred in Westminster Abbey.

Of the writer in old age, a great deal could be written. He seems to have been old when young, with the wary, self-protective reticence of a man ill at ease in his newfound milieu. Yet what affronted Victorian society in his portrayal of *Jude the Obscure* (and the foredoomed character of "Little Father Time") feels uneventful now. To *épater le bourgeois* was never his desire, since he desired membership in the moneyed bourgeoisie. The notion that an artist should be regular in personal behavior and scandalous in work is wholly apposite here; Hardy saved his daring for his art. Cautious in public demeanor, and trying to be "clubbable," he nonetheless contrived to shock by the unblinking rigor of his discussion of class and poverty and loss of faith; where Dickens managed to be charming, Hardy is relentless. By anatomizing bitterness, he fails where he succeeds.

And so he turns to poetry. He has never really turned from it, but now it's all he has. Some of it—"The Dynasts"—might as well have been prose fiction; the narrative sweep, the discursiveness, the theoretical superstructure all are outward facing in the mode of his second-rate novels. But the poems he wrote on the loss of his wife—the long haunted sequence of lyrics, where he offered to her memory what Emma claimed

he withheld in her lifetime: unmediated tender attention—are triumphs of unalloyed feeling. In poem after
poem, Hardy writes with grave simplicity about their
vanished youth. His elegy, "The Voice," was composed
in December 1912, a few weeks after her death:

Woman much missed, how you call to me, call to me,
Saying that now you are not as you were
When you had changed from the one who was all to me,
But as at first, when our day was fair.

A recent biographer, Claire Tomalin, claims Hardy's
late work is his most intimately expressive; in his seventies he wrote for, as it were, an audience of one. As
Tomalin describes it, "Only in poetry was there no com-
promising, and in the 'Poems of 1912–13' he bared his
heart as he had never fully allowed himself to do before.
It gives them their immediacy and power, allowing us to
eavesdrop on his train of thought and feeling as he moves
between an old man's sorrow and a young man's bliss."[2]

The last lines of "The Voice" are these:

Thus I, faltering forward,
Leaves around me falling,
Wind oozing thin through the thorn from norward,
And the woman calling.

• • •

Franz Joseph Haydn (1732–1809) was a titan of industry, a fount of music-making from the start. If Hardy in old age wrote "darkling" verse, the composer all his life retained what everyone reports on as his sunny disposition. Few other figures in the history of art have been so happily productive or so uncomplaining. But this was a function of character, not smiling prior circumstance; he was born neither to privilege nor a line of successful musicians. Much of his youth he went hungry. As Haydn said of his first teacher, Johann Mathias Frankh, "I shall be grateful to that man as long as I live for keeping me so hard at work, though I used to get more flogging than food."[3]

He himself became a teacher, of enduring influence throughout the musical canon. Mozart acknowledged great personal indebtedness; so too did Beethoven, and his list of students includes such major figures as Neukomm, Lessel, and Pleyel. His orchestral jokes and piano trios and soaring oratorios are inventive yet authoritative—technically agile as well as, in spirit, "composed." Haydn's importance in the literature cannot be overstated; from cello concerto to string quartet to symphony, he was both pioneer and settler, both innovative and exact.

The son of a wheelwright from the Austrian village

of Rohrau, Franz Joseph was the second of twelve children; by age six it was clear he had a "vocation" and by age eight he qualified as choirboy for the Viennese Cathedral. In 1759 Haydn found employment as the music director for Count Morzin in Vienna and the next year had sufficient resources to provide 1,000 guilden for marriage to Maria Anna Keller, a wig-maker's daughter. Thereafter he labored more or less uninterruptedly in the service of patrons, and it's worth remembering how crucial a role such patronage has played in the history of art. Now we have foundations and prizes and galleries and publishing houses, the whole apparatus of commerce; then there were wealthy and titled individuals who did the commissioning. Without such enabling, if self-interested, sponsorship we would have no Sistine Ceiling or Brandenburg Concertos or *Twelfth Night*; most of the great creative hallmarks of our Western culture have been undertaken for hire and, in effect, on command.

In 1761 Haydn became attached to the Esterházys, one of Hungary's richest and most powerful families. Prince Nikolaus I proved an amiable patron who, Haydn wrote, "approved all my works"; even the periods of isolation in the country retreats of the aristocratic Esterházys were a kind of blessing. Haydn had the freedom to "make experiments." He concludes, "I was set apart from the world, there was nobody in my vicinity to confuse and annoy me in my course, and so I had to be original."[4]

During his three decades of employment by the Esterházy family, the composer produced eleven operas, sixty symphonies, five masses, thirty sonatas, one concerto, and hundreds of brief works. After the prince's death, he journeyed to London and wrote on commission for the entrepreneur J. P. Salomon. While resident in England, "Father" Haydn—known to Austrians as "Papa"—created the resounding London Symphonies and major oratorios; *The Creation* (1798) and *The Seasons* (1801) are two of his finest achievements. In the end he returned to Vienna, much venerated there. His faith was as unwavering as his work ethic; both lasted all his life.

Of his final appearance at a performance of *The Creation*, on March 27, 1808, H. C. Robbins Landon has this to report:[5]

On the day appointed, Haydn was carried into the Great Hall to the sound of trumpet fanfares and tumultuous applause, and seated next to Princess Esterházy. The cream of Viennese society was there to pay a last public homage to the Father of the Symphony (as they thought him) and String Quartet. Salieri and Haydn embraced tenderly, surrounded by cheering crowds. Beethoven, the tears streaming down his face, bent and kissed the hand of his former teacher. When the passage, "And there was Light" was reached, Haydn (as Carpani, who was an eye-witness, relates) "raised his trembling arms to Heaven, as if in prayer to the Father of Harmony." At the end of the First Part, it was thought advisable to take Haydn home.

The next year, he would die.

•   •   •

The "Matisse Chapel" by Henri Matisse (1869–1954) occupies a site not far removed from the center of Vence, at the base of the Alpes Maritimes. With its narrow, twisting streets and stunted plane trees and traffic congestion, Vence is neither as picturesque as its near neighbor, St. Paul de Vence, nor as glamorous as Nice. I was twenty-one years old the first time I visited, and remember being bored. The old provincial city has an inward-facing aspect, even a kind of walled-in secretiveness, and that holds true for the chapel as well. Its exterior is unremarkable—modern, bright, squat—and little of its outward guise suggests the work within.

The day was wet. It was March. At this remove I can't remember what it was I thought I'd find: a Romanesque building, perhaps, or soaring Gothic edifice commensurate with the romantic story of Matisse's gift. According to that story, he made a promise to his young caregiver

Monique Bourgeois—soon to become a Dominican nun—that if he recovered he'd offer his thanks in the way he knew best: making art. The master had been very ill and no one was certain that he would survive. Mlle. Bourgeois, however, nursed her charge with skill and grace, and he did recover and in gratitude fashioned a chapel—not merely decorating it with stained-glass windows and an altar, but also designing the ciborium and robes and liturgical vestments to wear.

The first stone of the Rosaire Chapel was laid on December 12, 1949. On June 25, 1951, Monsignor Rémond consecrated the structure. By that time Matisse, unwell again, was unable to attend, so this proved to be a labor of the artist's final period, one of the last he achieved. But to the young man meandering through the small building it all seemed, somehow, perfunctory: a dull gray light, a few people praying, a window or two with designs.

I have been back often since, and the site has changed. It's not, of course, the thing viewed but the viewer that has altered over time; by now the chapel seems to me a marvel of exuberant restraint. More and more in his decline the painter used material susceptible to lightsome touch: the *découpages* that others would render as mosaics, the stained-glass windows that others would fashion, the chasubles others would weave. Yet he oversaw every detail; his charcoal and oil studies are extensive. For the figure of Saint Dominic or image of the Virgin and Child there are quantities of sketches— sheet after sheet. The Stations of the Cross, filling most of the nave's east wall, might well have felt self-reflexive as burden; he labored on them painfully, repeatedly, rearranging them obsessively to the very last.

It overstates the case to say Matisse refused to die because he wanted to provide a space where his young friend might worship in a contemporary version of the ancient Dominican way. But there is something both timely and timeless about *Le Rosaire*, and it feels like a promise delivered. When light shines through the windows here, a great deal is illumined; religious faith and the art which honors it become one and the same.

His grandchildren would remember paying a visit to the family patriarch lying in bed. Matisse would take a bamboo pole, affix a charcoal to its tip, and draw their portraits on the ceiling. As Paul Matisse, his grandson, recalls: "He didn't just look at me and take in the appearance I exhibited. Instead, his eyes seemed to project a powerful light of his own invention upon me.... It was only when he finally focused on the desired image that he began to draw."[6]

If Picasso incarnates the creative personality for whom change is crucial, Henri Matisse (like Franz Joseph Haydn or, in his own field, Georges Braque and Paul Cézanne) embraced a kind of constancy; the arc of his career is more a straight than a jagged line. What fascinated the apprentice continued to intrigue the master; the twenty- and eighty-year-old seem two sides of the one coin. Matisse was not religious in the formal sense, but his profession was a faith to which he stayed committed. The structure of the chapel enforced a kind of union between his exploration of the plane and the three-dimensionality of architecture; the artist in old age remained compelled by the play of shape, color, and light.

· · ·

My uncle, an art dealer, drove me to meet Henry Moore (1898–1986). More precisely, he had a meeting at Hoglands, Moore's house outside of London, and asked if I'd care to accompany him; I had been working in his gallery and was glad to go. We drove through a wet countryside, and there was snow on the ground. Henry and Irina Moore moved to the village of Much Hadham, Hertfordshire, in 1940; they had been living in Hampstead, where my uncle also lived, but their house off Trasker Road was damaged in the Blitz. Slowly, steadily, the couple enlarged and improved the property at Hoglands, turning outbuildings into studios and planting a fine garden. By the time I visited in 1964 it had become a considerable establishment—if not as grand and photogenic as would later be the case. Chocka-block with art (both of Moore's making and by him collected), it had a ramshackle beauty—a low brown roof, brick chimneys—and the lived-in feel of rooms not furnished for display. A Courbet oil hung catercorner to a Dan mask and a dancing figure by Rodin; there were books and bottles everywhere, shelves filled with *objets trouvés.*

The artist's wife, Irina, and their daughter, Mary, made the two of us welcome inside. My uncle and the sculptor accomplished their shared business; then there was tea. When, briefly, snow stopped falling, Moore took us on a ramble down the garden paths and, mid-sentence, paused and, stooping, considered the shape of a stone. The gesture seemed habitual. Whether or not he intended to make an impression and did this routinely with guests, I've never forgotten that practiced glance, the way he stopped and examined and then pocketed the rock. On the instant, or so it seemed to me, an accident of nature became—because *seen*—a work of art.

Behind the main house, and prominently visible, rose a plastic tent. It ballooned around the plaster model-in-progress for a figure which, once cast in bronze, would be transported to Manhattan's Lincoln Center. This sculpture fashioned by an English artist was to be cast at a German foundry and transported by freighter to the harbor of New York. Now it sits in a reflecting pool, with concert- and theatergoers hurrying past; then there were ladders and space heaters and steps incised in the high body of the burgeoning object on which the senior sculptor (though he was strong and agile, still, in his mid-sixties) and assistants labored. It was too sizeable to be positioned inside Moore's maquette studio and loomed like a white behemoth beneath the polyethylene sheeting on which snow puddled, melting. He would work on it all winter long.

In conversation and in his writings, Moore had an unforced eloquence. Here is a kind of credo, from his unpublished notes for "A View of Sculpture" (1950):[7]

> You see, I think a sculptor is a person who is interested in the shape of things. A poet is somebody who is interested in words; a musician is someone who is interested in or obsessed by sounds. But a sculptor is a person obsessed with the form and the shape of things, and it's not just the shape of any one thing, but the shape of anything and everything: the growth of a flower, the hard, tense strength, although delicate form of a bone; the strong, solid fleshiness of a beech tree trunk. All these things are just as much a lesson to a sculptor as a pretty girl.... It's as though you have something trying to make itself come to a shape from inside itself. This is, perhaps, what makes me interested in bones as much as in flesh because the bone is the inner structure of all living form.

Of the aging artist, Donald Hall has this to say: "When I saw Moore the year he turned eighty, I asked him, in a jocular manner I hope, to tell me the secret of life. Without jocularity he answered that the secret was to devote yourself entirely to one end, to one goal, and to work every day toward this goal, to put all your energy and imagination into the one endeavor. The only necessity was that this goal be unattainable."[8]

•   •   •

Alice Neel (1900–1984) remained unflinching, gimlet eyed. A portrait painter all her life, she trained her gaze—in one of her last portraits—on her own old naked body. She is sitting heavily, encased in a blue-and-white-striped armchair, holding a rag and a brush. There is no easel, no palette to hand. She displays no jewelry, no ornamentation beyond—perhaps—lipstick; her lips are a deep red. Her coiffed hair is white; she wears glasses; the floor beneath her seems, improbably enough, both ocher and light green. The shadows of the chair legs and the shadows on the wall are the same blue as the fabric of the armchair and the skin of her right calf. That blue appears elsewhere as well. The space suggests a living room rather than a studio, the sort of chair one sits in when company arrives. It is not an artist's stool. As she had written earlier:[9]

I do not know if the truth that I have told will benefit the world in any way. I managed to do it at great cost to myself and perhaps to others. It is hard to go against the tide of one's time, milieu, and position....

I always was much more truthful and courageous on canvas.

She had painted nudes before, and several pregnant women, their bellies and their pubic hair proudly on display. This is not that. Her breasts are pendulous, her stomach distended, the flesh both full and slack. The artist and the artist's model equally are focused on the picture we here have. One eyebrow is raised, one toe also; she stares out at the viewer as if looking at the canvas reflected in a mirror, the mirror she must use in order to complete this very image. Painters have been doing so since the time of Albrecht Dürer, but seldom when wearing no clothes. The eyes are dark, white pupils large, imperfectly aligned. She studies herself as we study her self-scrutiny—preparing to make an adjustment, to add a daub of color or shift perspective slightly?—and in that reflected glare we see what Daniel Martin (in John Fowles's eponymous novel) saw in Rembrandt's self-portrait in Kenwood: "whole sight."

It is 1980; the artist is eighty years old. That year she wrote, "The minute I sat in front of a canvas, I was happy. Because it was a world, and I could do as I liked in it."[10] In previous years this had also been true, but there were elements of protest and an embrace of bohemian life. Brought up in what she thought of as the confines of small-town America, she moved to New York, partnered a series of husbands and lovers, read widely, and wrote well on politics and painting, doing her work against the grain—or at least on the perimeter—of contemporary fashion. "Lettering, for example, seemed important to Neel for what it said, not for the shape of the letters."[11] In later life she became a celebrity, much honored by the cultural and political establishment, given medals and solo exhibitions and appearing on *The Johnny Carson Show.* Her portraits of fellow artists and poets (Allen Ginsberg, Marisol, Frank O'Hara, Faith Ringgold, Robert Smithson, the Soyer brothers, Annie Sprinkle, Andy Warhol) and art critics and historians (Henry Geldzahler, Meyer Schapiro) attest to the glad company she kept.

Neel celebrated the nameless as well: children, couples, families, and those needing handouts or working in clinics. Years before, her sketches had been decorous—reticent, even, as daughter or mother—but now there seems no point in scarves or wall hangings or anything beyond the flat unvarnished fact. What beauty she claims is the beauty of age; what she represents is survival. We call it "naked truth." If one is fortunate enough to live this long, and sit in a well-heated room, artistic implement in hand, it needn't be dispiriting; more nearly the reverse. She had painted the young and the glamorous often; she herself was both of these but is beyond vanity now. A final photograph—taken by Robert Mapplethorpe, who visited the artist days before her death from cancer at the age of eighty-four—shows the same indomitable face above a clothed and wasted body: *jolie laide.* "Death thou shalt die."

● ● ●

George Sand (1804–1876) was the most successful female author of nineteenth-century France. Like Mme. De Staël before her, and Colette thereafter, she used her wit to skewer the society of which she was a celebrated member, remaining *engagée* until the very end. It's difficult to delimit the reach of her enthusiasms or the impact of her public role; she was volcanic and unstoppable and—no better word for it—*smart.* What claimed her attention was more or less everything, and about it all she had opinions trenchantly expressed.

In her last years, however, she withdrew from politics and Paris, living on the estate, Nohant, that had been her childhood home. There she shared her retreat with visitors like Gustave Flaubert and Ivan Turgenev. (Earlier, she had had love affairs with artists such as Alfred de Musset and Frédéric Chopin.) With Flaubert she maintained an impassioned correspondence about politics and art as well the pleasures of grandparental life; he called her his *chère bon maître,* she called him *cher vieux troubadour.* The letters of these writers (as translated by Francis Steegmuller and Barbara Bray) are a delight. Elegantly quarreling with Flaubert's artistic credo, she asserts:[12]

> I know you disapprove of personal attitudes entering into literature. But are you right? Isn't your stand due to lack of conviction rather than aesthetic principle?...It seems to me that your school of writers fails to concern itself with the depths, and tends too much to stay on the surface. By dint of striving after form it underrates content. It addresses itself to a literary audience. But that audience doesn't really exist, as such. We are human beings before we are anything else.

If Aurore Dupin lived a conventional life, she got it out of the way early. There was the childhood in the countryside, a few years at a convent finishing school, a marriage at eighteen to a baron's son nine years her senior, and motherhood just shy of nineteen. Even in these early years, however, there are hints of the revolutionary and literary figure she would become: sparks of youthful rebellion, a penchant for male dress, an interest in the work of physician's assistant, and a love affair with the man who tutored her in anatomy.[13]

One of her first works, undertaken jointly with her lover Julien Sandeau, was praised by Balzac; *Valentine*, her second solo novel under the *nom de plume* of George Sand, was written in only two months. This foreshadows the enormous productivity that would characterize her long career: some sixty novels and twenty plays between 1830 and 1876. Further, she published short stories and political and literary essays, as well as her massive autobiography, *Histoire de Ma Vie* (serialized in 138 installments from 1854 to 1855 in the Paris newspaper *La Presse*). At its best, her fiction has both urgency and fluency; her characters are vivid and her plotting fine. It has been claimed she wrote too much, too fast, but the creation of "George Sand" herself was an important invention, and what she propounds is undaunted belief "in the necessity of goodness and beauty."[14] It was her clarion call.

As a biographer reports, "Certain things about Sand did not change, even as she lived into her eighth decade: the relentless enjoyment of tobacco, the habit of writing late into the night, and dips in the River Indre, against the strict advice of her doctors. Even at the time of her death in 1876, she was at work on both the novel, *Albine*, and *Contes d'une Grand-mère,* a collection meant to encourage her grandchildren to read."[15]

What stands out here is energy, a passionate asser-tiveness that powered her behavior from the start. Both as precursor and model of the "liberated woman," she is easy to admire and very hard to dismiss. Here are some lines she sent Flaubert from Nohant on January 12, 1876, five months before her death:[16]

> Everyone sees things from his own point of view, which I acknowledge should be chosen freely. I can summarize my own point of view in a few words: not to stand in front of a misted window which shows one nothing but the reflection of one's own nose. And to see as much as possible—good, evil, near, far, around, about; and to perceive how every-thing, tangible or intangible, constantly gravitates towards the necessity of goodness, kindness, truth and beauty.

• • •

Clara Schumann (1819–1896) too was attached to men of genius: principal among them her husband, Robert Schumann, and his protégé, Johannes Brahms. Turn by turn she played the roles of student, lover, wife and helpmate, teacher, impresario, breadwinner, mother, muse. During her lifetime, moreover (or at any rate its early years), she was *the* acclaimed musician of her circle: the celebrated prodigy and pianoforte-playing virtuoso, Clara Wieck Schumann. At age nine she first appeared with orchestras and at eleven offered her first solo concert, debuting in Leipzig's famed *Gewandhaus* in 1830, and playing thereafter for Goethe in Weimar. By thirteen she was enjoying a full-fledged career and performing showy repertoire pieces by Kalkbrenner, Herz, Henselt, and Czerny as well as the compositions of the new Romantics, Chopin, Mendelssohn, and her inamorata, Schumann. Later she became a major interpreter of the work of past composers—Scarlatti, Bach, Mozart, Beethoven, and Schubert among them—by the public much applauded and, by Brahms, adored.

Friedrich Wieck opposed the marriage of his daughter to the unstable Schumann and did everything in his power to prevent it. The story of the couple's passionate affair and Robert's incremental madness is a sad one, well worth telling; her husband spent his final years in the asylum of Endenich while Clara concertized in order to earn what she needed to keep their large household afloat.[17] Most of the family income was hers; most of the audience flocked to hear Clara, not Robert, and when she gave her farewell concert in Frankfurt in March of 1891 she had been onstage for more than sixty years.

The mother of seven surviving children, Clara Wieck Schumann stopped composing when only thirty-six. But her Piano Trio in G Minor (1846) and the 1853 Romances for violin and piano (which she wrote for

Robert's birthday and dedicated to Joseph Joachim, who performed them for George V of Hanover) are first-rate compositions, and her preludes, fugues, and *pièces fugitives* all merit attention today. Such songs as *"Die stille Lotusblume"* and *"Liebst du um Schönheit"* have a crystalline effectiveness, and it's hard to know precisely why she ceased to write. As she put it in her diary, "Composing gives me great pleasure.... There is nothing which surpasses the joy of creation, if only because through it one wins hours of self-forgetfulness, when one lives in a world of sound."[18] Yet as early as the age of twenty, she confessed, "I once thought that I possessed creative talent, but I have given up this idea. A woman must not desire to compose—not one has been able to do it, and why should I expect to?"[19]

It's possible that her association with Mendelssohn, Schumann, and Brahms proved daunting to an artist who construed her own gifts modestly; it's possible she thought herself—as suggested above—no more than merely competent. Her father taught her to compose as part of her musical education, not as an occupation in and of itself. As was the case for Fanny Mendelssohn and her more famous brother, the burden of expectation would have been lodged elsewhere. Nor should one underestimate the claims of daily duty. Her husband's romantic importuning, her children's fiscal and physical needs, her father's angry disavowal and her (perhaps platonic) lover Brahms's adulatory proximity, the concert and travel schedule she maintained, her authoritative editing of Robert's works for the publishing firm of Breitkopf & Härtel, his suicide attempts, their immense correspondence, the pressures of fame—all these would have kept Clara Schumann from the composer's desk.

But whatever the reason or reasons, her own creative energy flourished at the keyboard. As one of her admirers put it:[20]

> Her playing was characterized by an entire absence of personal display, a keen perception of the composer's meaning, and an unfailing power of setting it forth in perfectly intelligible form. These qualities would lead one to pronounce her one of the most intellectual of players, were it not that that term has come to imply a certain coldness or want of feeling, which was never perceived in her playing.

The child prodigy in later years is a special subset of *Lastingness,* and Clara Wieck had been a virtuoso almost from the start. Young performers as they age can be self-aggrandizing as well as self-destructive, but this artist when mature retained a kind of modesty. Like Claudio Arrau, Yehudi Menuin, and Yo-Yo Ma (to pick three more recent virtuosos of the instruments for which she wrote her piano trio), she served music first and last.

• • •

It is, of course, the railway station in November: his death in Astapovo. It is the image that compels me of an old man on a wooden bench refusing to go home. Count Lev Nikolayevich Tolstoy (1828–1910) spent his last days in the stationmaster's house of a provincial village while trying to escape. He would not have put it that way; he would have called it one stage of a quest, the act of renunciation by which honest elders retreat. But what we have are photos of a fierce white-bearded peasant with the aristocratic mien he cannot quite relinquish—the boots are too good, the blanket too soft, the worldwide attention too keen. His gaze is both piercing and rapt.

And there's an aspect of low comedy as well as high seriousness here. This is an extract from his wife, Sofia's journal the day after Tolstoy fled:[21]

> ...On October 28, at 5 in the morning, Lev Nik. slipped out of the house with D.P. Makovitsky. His excuse for leaving was that I had been rummaging through his papers the previous night. I had gone into his study for a moment, but I did not touch one paper—indeed there *weren't* any papers on his desk. In his letter to me (written for the entire world) the pretext he gave was our luxurious life and his desire to be alone and to live in a hut like the peasants....

When I learnt from Sasha and the letter about L.N.'s flight, I jumped into the pond in despair. Sasha and Bulgakov got me out, alas!

Around the world they read and read of him; on his estates they pray for him; in a private railroad car, having followed him from Yasnaya Polyana, his wife curses and blesses her renegade L.N. while he tosses on the interrupted journey he thinks of as a pilgrimage, proceeding from title to title of the books he'd composed: *Childhood. Boyhood. Youth. The Cossacks. The Death of Ivan Ilyich. What Then Must We Do?*

For much of his life he embraced what he loathed and loathed what he embraced. The dialectic is his mode, a synthesis of opposites: Tolstoy the warrior-pacifist and ascetic voluptuary, the profligate bachelor turned doting parent, a prodigal son who fathered nine children, a cosmopolite and laborer at work in the fields of his lordship who was himself the lord. The final ruckus he occasioned while hunting isolation feels characteristic, somehow: his arrogant humility, his self-abasing pride. *Anna Karenina. Resurrection. The Three Hermits. War and Peace.*

So it's perhaps not surprising that he made an opposition of the claims of art and life. As of 1891 Tolstoy renounced his copyright royalties, and in *What Is Art?* (1898) proclaimed his own early work worthless;

indeed, the whole enterprise of art itself was savaged by its magisterial practitioner. His diatribe denounced—or rendered moot—all that he had done before, the great books he had written. Here's an extract from his diary, written on July 19, 1896:[22]

> ...I plainly saw that all this music and fiction and poetry is not art, that men do not have the slightest need for it, that it is nothing but a distraction for profiteers and idlers, that it has nothing to do with life. Novels and short stories describe the revolting manner in which two creatures become infatuated with each other; poems explain and glorify how to die of boredom; and music does the same. And all the while life, all of life, is beating at us with urgent questions—food, the distribution of property, labor, religion, human relations! It's a shame! It is ignoble! Help me, Father, to serve you by destroying falsehood.

A Confession. Conjugal Happiness. On Life. The Kreutzer Sonata. Had he been willing to follow his own good advice, much might have been avoided. "Conversations don't help to establish good relations," wrote Tolstoy, "on the contrary they damage them. We should talk as little as possible, especially with those we set store by."[23] When he fled Yasnaya Polyana it was for the sake of "peace and solitude," but relatives and hangers-on and the chatter of the telegraph surrounded him nevertheless. And when at last they buried him on his estate, it was in a grove of the forest where—according to his elder brother's story—a green stick had been hidden, with a formula engraved on it for universal love.

• • •

Ralph Vaughan Williams (1872–1958), like Franz Joseph Haydn, made music till the end. His almost exact coeval, Jean Sibelius (1865–1957) went silent the last thirty years of his life; though he was rumored to be working, always working, on his eighth symphony, it never has been heard. The English composer, however—who dedicated his own fifth symphony to Sibelius—kept rendering irrelevant each retrospective judgment. In 1937 music critic Frank Stewart Howes was the first to pronounce a premature postmortem; when Howes published the little volume, *The Later Works of R. Vaughan Williams,* his subject had two full decades of accomplishment remaining.[24]

Following the fifth symphony (1943) came the Symphony in E Minor in 1948. If Vaughan Williams had "summed up his life's philosophy in the characteristic and perhaps retrospective fifth symphony," the sixth showed him "at the age of 76 with all the assurance of mastery starting off once more into uncharted regions of thought."[25] In each of the years 1953, 1956, and 1958 he produced additional examples of the form, bringing the life total up to nine, more than twice the number extant when Howes wrote of later Williams. And even in his eighties—when working on the cantata *Epithalamion,* the *Ten Blake Songs,* the *Variations for Brass Band,* and the beginning of a three-act opera, *Thomas the Rhymer*—this Janus-faced composer started out anew.

Like Tolstoy or Thomas Hardy (whose *Tess of the D'Urbervilles* hovers in the background of his ninth and final symphony), Vaughan Williams was a figure of self-contradiction. His music belongs to the twentieth century, but much of it would seem congenial to a sixteenth-century musician and, indeed, that era's audience. The "folksy" evocation of cow pastures and country lanes comes from a pen (his handwriting was abysmal, perhaps because, though a natural left-hander, he wrote with his right hand) that scored a fistful of films. A socialist who turned down a knighthood and twice refused to become Master of the King's Musick, he happily wrote fanfares for two coronations; the "determined atheist" Williams edited the *English Hymnal* and was avowedly inspired by religious themes. As with the backward-facing adaptation of the *Tallis Fantasia,* or his use of folk songs, he was rooted in English tradition, yet composers as modern and dissimilar as Bartók and Rachmaninoff greatly admired the work. The Second

String Quartet (1943), to take just a single example, is both anguished in the mode of Shostakovitch and, in its epilogue, serene. Now, more than fifty years after his death, his reputation enlarges; the whiff of critical condescension that can accompany popular success has by and large disappeared.

His first wife, Adeline, died in 1951. For much of their shared life, Adeline's presence and her immobility (induced by a crippling arthritis) was Williams's magnetic north. All journeys had been short; he had planned exactly how long he would be away at festivals, and his absences had been as brief as possible. Now he began to spend more time in London with his longtime lover (and eventual second wife and biographer) Ursula Wood. Williams and Ursula—who lived till ninety-six, dying in 2007—traveled. The list of destinations is impressive: In 1952 a trip to France included stops in Paris, St. Malo, and Rouen; 1953 saw their wedding, followed by a holiday in Italy. In 1954, professing a desire to see the Grand Canyon, Williams used a lecture tour and a visiting professorship at Cornell as an excuse to travel the United States.[26]

As the years pass, the composer's posture grows more hunched, his leaning upon Ursula ever more pronounced. A hearing aid is a fixture after 1954,[27] but a 1956 photo shows him with baton in hand, conducting "The Lark Ascending" and looking as focused and exacting as ever. That work was written in 1914, its lyric melancholy somehow presaging England's entry into all-leveling battle; the sixth symphony records the anguish of his homeland after the Second World War.

• • •

What way to uncover the secrets of growth? There is no single answer to that simple question. If "Bodily decrepitude is wisdom," as William Butler Yeats observed, these men and women each attained a kind of wisdom at or near the end. I conclude this series of brief long lives with an image of the bespectacled composer, his hair rumpled, tie askew, in the company of players who are paying close attention to the pages of a score. *Andante,* he seems to be telling them, *lento, piu lento, lentissimo* here.

CHAPTER FOUR

"Each Day I Am Reborn"

All the new thinking is about loss.
In this, it resembles all the old thinking. . . .
Robert Hass
"Meditation at Lagunitas"

In this and two subsequent chapters, I do intend to go, if not *lentissimo,* slow. I examine the careers of nine exemplary figures—musicians, writers, painters—who persisted with their labors in old age. The first and last examples are extreme: a German poet whose decline was steep, an Italian novelist whose ascent was equally so. In between come instances of less dramatic change: writers, painters, and musicians who continued with their chosen form until their lives were

93

done. Each chapter contains three portraits, one for each of the three modes. In the sequence of these sketches—not full-dress, but detailed—I try to describe what kept them engaged as creative artists and of what their late style consists. Identity is various as well as mutable; there are nine different stories to tell.

• • •

The great German poet Johann Christian Friedrich Hölderlin (1770–1843) spent half his life in Tübingen; mad, he was watched over by the carpenter in town. During his life he had scant recognition; in the productive period (from, roughly, 1794 to 1805) his work ran ahead of the curve. More modern practitioners such as Rilke and Celan derive descent from Hölderlin, but at the time he had few followers and a diminishing number of friends. When he made an admirer's pilgrimage to Johann Wolfgang von Goethe, that arbiter of excellence showed him to the door.

The house now known as Hölderlin's was not, accordingly, one he owned; he stayed incarcerate there. I first walked past that structure as many years ago—thirty-six—as he was locked inside it; I went again last year. Let me describe it in the present tense, since my topic's "lastingness," and the view's unchanged. With its slate-roofed conical tower, the house sits at the end of a little allée, and in it the poet languished from 1807 on.

Wooden boats lie clustered at the River Neckar's edge; boatmen punt lovers through bridges and up and down the brown reach. "Hölderlin's *Turm*" or "tower" is yellow, its garden green, and plane trees are established on the farther bank.

Now the site has become a museum, open some hours each week. When I arrive there is a clutch of students being lectured in the "library"; at the stroke of noon they leave. On the second floor it's possible to listen, on headsets, to Heinz Holliger's settings of Hölderlin songs. Once, a closed door opens and a woman emerges, bearing an armload of books. She sees me, says *"Grüss Gott,"* and retreats. For the next hour, I wander alone, and the house seems near-eerily quiet; I am the single paying visitor, and the gray-haired custodian reads a magazine.

There's little noise of traffic here: only the river, the chatter of boatmen, the wind. Comfort would have been available to Hölderlin in this circular enclosure; long confinement in a tower would have kept him, if nothing else, safe. The carpenter Ernst Zimmer became the poet's landlord; when this scrupulous caretaker died— some thirty years thereafter—his daughter Lotte took over the role. *Zimmer* means "room" in German, and the space does feel echoic: Zimmer's Hölderlin's *Zimmer* is empty except for a pair of stiff-backed wooden chairs, as well as four framed verses on the walls. The seasons—Spring, Summer, Fall, Winter—are adduced by the poet in rhyming quatrains; contemporary artwork lines the halls.

The biographical sheet dispensed in the museum is succinct. *"Verschlimmerung von Hölderlin's Zustand"*— "Worsening of Hölderlin's Condition"—is the tagline for 1805. The Autenrieth clinic they sent him to in Tübingen was supposed to be the most modern of facilities, and inmates were prescribed digitalis and belladonna: drugs that might have been of use. But they also offered the "Autenrieth mask," used to stop patients from screaming; there were forcible immersions in cold water and, of course, the straitjacket. Hölderlin was treated for the physical ailment of scabies, then pronounced incurable in terms of psychic ailment and given three years to live. It was no doubt fortunate the authorities released him; one of his fellow patients died of the treatment received.

Who knows if modern medication could have alleviated the poet's *Wahnsinn* or controlled his madness; today he might be functional and sitting in a classroom or a boardroom, popping pills. Some have called into question the whole diagnosis; there was estrangement from his family, who kept him in near poverty although his inheritance would have been large. He had trouble finding and keeping employment; his beloved Susette Gontard (married to another man, with children) died.

He was, it would seem, prone to fits of enthusiasm, anger, and despondency—but that holds true for many now who are not locked away.

"Apollon hat mich geschlagen" is the line he uttered when returning from a walking tour, insane. "Apollo has struck me!" Or, alternatively, "stricken me." What more appropriate phrase for an artist of the Enlightenment, and one in love with Greece? Less romantically, perhaps, he was describing sunstroke; when you order coffee *mit Schlag* you ask for a dab of whipped cream. In a letter written as early as November 1802, Hölderlin told his friend Casimir Ulrich Böhlendorff: "The mighty element, the fire of heaven and the silence of the people, their life in nature, their confinedness and their contentment, moved me continually, and as one says of heroes, I can well say of myself that Apollo has struck me."[1]

He was invaded, it would seem, by that harsh lyre-thwacking god, and no diet or emetic or blood-letting permitted him to enter the daily round again. For whatever the true diagnosis and whatever the cause of his madness, he lived out his life in this space. (There's a long list of prison writings, the *De Profundis Clamavi* of those who are confined and make in that confinement an enduring work of art. But Hölderlin is no Boethius or Cervantes or Jean Genet or Oscar Wilde, who wrote *De Profundis* while in Reading Gaol; he's a man of muddled mind producing doggerel.) Too, Hölderlin grew reconciled; we have no episodes of howling or head-bashing as part of tower lore. I imagine him fashioning handwritten scraps—signing them *Scardanelli*, his delusional alter ego—and making paper planes of rhyme to fling at the neighborhood children. The wide wooden planks have been sanded and varnished; there's no trace of pacing feet or fingernail incisions on the wall.

If "We poets in our youth begin in gladness," and decline thereafter in "despondency and madness,"[2] it's, by convention, a rapid decline. The candle flames, then sputters out; the meteor crashes to earth. Chatterton, Keats, Rimbaud, Plath: Each in their several ways describe a quick trajectory, and Keats of course was consumptive—another scourge of gifted youth—not mad. But the image of a poet gone insane or suicidal seems connected to an early death, and there's something doubly sorrowful about an old man (in 1843 a seventy-three-year-old would have been ancient) parsing and scribbling out rhyme after rhyme.

Of course the neighbors laughed. Of course the critics scoffed. The verse he composed was at first labeled nonsense (if only by comparison with the language of "Hyperion," "Empedocles," and other early efforts); all intricate complexity was ironed out by pain. Here's an example from his final years:[3]

The comforting things of this world I enjoyed,
But my hours of youth have been long since destroyed,
April and May and July are far gone,
I'm nothing now, not happy to live on!

No matter how poignant the sentiment here, there's very little art. This sort of easy rhyming and Hallmark-card simplicity is far removed from his previous work, the long lines and elaborate associations of the "Odes" and "Epigrams" and "Hymns" or celebrations of "Socrates and Alcibiades" and "Rousseau." The poet who walked "the Philosophers' Way" in Heidelberg and studied Greek and Latin at four o'clock each morning had his attention span reduced if not obliterated; what's left is pathos and mild piety. Nevertheless, and continually, out of old habit he wrote. He had a gift; he lost it; the melody was muted, then went flat.

So I think of Friedrich Hölderlin spending thirty-six years upstairs in the house, imagining himself on Parnassus, Olympus, and watching Apollo wheel past. The singer abandoned by song.

• • •

A coda here. For reasons that defy explanation, I have always found four-leaf clovers, and find them without trouble. I can be walking or jogging and a four-leaf clover fairly shouts at me, outlining itself in the lawn. I'm no good at sighting birds in trees or constellations in the nighttime sky, but four-leaf clovers shape themselves in the foreground of my vision, and with no conscious effort; I find many every year. What's more, the gift is inherited; my father found four-leaf clovers easily, and his mother did so before. Family history has it that my grandmother had amassed a hundred or so clovers in an envelope on her writing desk. And then her best friend's husband died, and she wrote and sealed a condolence note and left it on the desk. Returning after breakfast, she picked up the wrong envelope, addressed and sent it on. So when my grandmother's friend opened her mail the next morning, four-leaf clovers tumbled out. Which ruined not only the friendship but also Granny's collection.

·The man at the museum desk suggests I visit Hölderlin's garden, unlocking the door. I do this with real pleasure. The day is cool, with threats of rain; a boatman maneuvers past. I look down at him, then at my feet.

And there, above the waterline, by the parapet I lean on, are clovers in abundance: two five-leaf clovers first—problematic, since some believe the luck they bring, as for the poet, can be bad—then ten or twelve four-leaf clovers, with all the good fortune entailed. I pluck a handful of these trophies and offer them to the custodian; he's enthralled. *"Wunderbar,"* he says.

"*Unmöglich. Ach, das ist prachtvoll.*" I assure him it *is* possible, not wonderful or remarkable, and that he's welcome to—is in some sense the rightful possessor of—the luck. When luck left Friedrich Hölderlin, he wrote *moon* and *June* and *soon* and *spoon* (or their equivalents in German: *Sturm, Turm, Drang, sang*) in a Tower of Babel–like babble until the very end.

We shake hands. I leave.

• • •

This example of a poet dead two centuries ago seems a specter of depletion neither genre nor time bound. When the Wheel of Fortune spins, it does so for us all. Hölderlin's life was split in two—the first half kinetic, the second inert—but there are many others where the pattern looks less obvious and the collapse less extreme. We *peak* or *crest* or find ourselves at *the top of our game;* then comes the slow subtraction.

The lament for "poets in our youth" was composed by William Wordsworth, a writer longer lived than most of his coevals. His phrase refers to Thomas "Chatterton, the marvelous boy" (who died impoverished, a suicide at seventeen), and carries with it somewhere a whiff of satisfaction in the sheer fact of survival. The almost equally long-lived Robert Browning took Wordsworth to task for having abandoned his outsider status: "Just for a handful of silver he left us / Just for a riband to put in his coat."[4] And it's possible to argue that the "split" in Wordsworth—remarkable work achieved while young, tedious poetasting when old—is in its own way extreme; he died successful, not outcast or imprisoned, but his talent was depleted long before.

Wordsworth died at eighty, Browning at seventy-seven, and the problem posed is similar: How might one best continue? It isn't a matter of the quantity of work produced, though the prodigious output of some elder artists engenders admiration almost irrespective of quality. Rather, it touches the wellsprings of growth. What lasts; what fails to; why? Why should it happen so seldom for a poet such as Hölderlin that day's end appears pellucid as the dawn? Is it a function of habit, merely—and like most habits harder to break than to make? Is it a kind of addiction, and can such work at least provide the comfort of routine? And for those who retain their productive work ethic, as in the following two examples, what adjustments must be made? For in the original act of creation ("In the beginning was the Word…"), even the archetypal creator rested "on the seventh day."

• • •

Pablo Casals was born in the village of Vendrell near Barcelona on December 29, 1876; by the time of his death in Puerto Rico, nearly a century later, he was honored all over the world. On October 22, 1973, when Casals at length expired, his career had come to signify unremitting devotion to art; often he said of himself that he was old in years but young when he picked up a cello or the conductor's baton. "Diminuendo is the life of music,"[5] he observed, and though diminution might mean loss of bodily agility it did not attach to the mode of expression itself. At a concert canceled by rain in New York's Central Park, he took the microphone to say, "I am perhaps the oldest musician in the world. I am an old man, but in many senses I am a very young man."[6] Then, at the age of ninety-six, he exhorted his audience "to say things to the world that are true. Goodness, love—this is the real world. Let us have love, love and peace."[7]

As with the cellist Mstislav Rostropovich (who died in 2007 at a mere eighty and whose father was once Casals's student), the life of music and the life of politics were, for the performer, intertwined. Each used his eminence as artist to mount a podium and make positions heard. Rostropovitch publicly opposed the autocratic excess of the Soviet Union, though he loved his "Mother Russia" and is buried there. Casals's ashes were transported to his homeland only after Franco's death and, by the terms of his will, once Catalonia became an autonomous self-governing territory. (Another famed Pablo—Picasso—did much the same with *Guernica*, also rejecting all commerce with his native Spain.) This opposition to totalitarianism seems as enduring a hallmark of the "Maestro" as was the cello itself; his refusal to play for Hitler and Franco constitutes a sounding silence, and he became as much admired for his withdrawal from the concert stage as for his appearances on it. The moral force of Casals's position made him a symbol of resistance, revered by those who had no prior interest in Boccherini or Dvořák; when he played for President Kennedy or at the United Nations, he did so as a warrior for peace.

Yet he began, of course, as a performer, establishing a reputation that still holds nonpareil. This virtuoso of the cello had more to do with its popularity than any other individual in the instrument's long history; all contemporary players honor Casals's memory—much as they praise Stradivari as the supreme luthier. With Alfred Cortot and Jacques Thibaud, he made the piano trio a chamber music ensemble now comparable in importance to the string quartet. From relative anonymity within the orchestra, the violoncello has emerged as a solo instrument rivaling the piano and the violin, and this rise in consequence is more or less coeval with Casals's career. (Andrés Segovia did something similar for the classical guitar, and there are those who popularized the French horn and the flute.) While performers such as Rostropovich and Yo-Yo Ma have enlarged the instrument's audience, no player has done more to render its literature current, and Casals himself introduced as concert piece what most musicians think of as the alpha and omega of the repertoire: the Six Suites for Unaccompanied Violoncello by Johann Sebastian Bach. His discovery thereof has assumed the dimensions of myth, and is worth reporting:[8]

On one occasion in 1890, before he was fourteen, Pablo and his father were strolling in the little streets near the harbour, and entered a small music shop in the Carrer Ancha to look for new pieces to perform at the Café. Browsing among the manuscripts, they came across...a battered Grützacher edition of Bach's Six Suites for Unaccompanied Violoncello. It was the crucial musical discovery of Casals' life... when he got the score home and began to work through the Suites, he realized he had found the music that was closest to his soul:

"I began playing them with indescribable excitement. They became my most cherished music....I was thirteen at the time, but for the following eighty years the wonder of my discovery has continued to grow on me. Those suites opened up a whole new world."

Those "eighty years" have been much celebrated in biographies and captured in photo and film. As chamber

musician and soloist, his discography, from Bach to
Wagner, bulks large; his recording career extended
from 1915 until 1973. (Casals further claimed, though
this has not been substantiated, to have recorded with
the violinist Eugène Ysaÿe as early as 1904.) He began
conducting when young, and did so for most of his life.
So too was he a pianist and composer; his list of compositions is a long one, and "*El Cant des Ocells*" ("The Song
of the Birds"), a Medieval Catalan folk song he adapted
for the cello, is played now all over the world. It's not
the purpose of this study to consider his achievement in
detail: the years of performance, the years of exile, the
years in Puerto Rico and at the Festival Casals. Suffice
it to say that for decades he and his violoncello were
everywhere emblazoned as emblems of high art.

Yet the cello is an unforgiving instrument; intonation fails. A string player (as is the case for a horn player)
must *produce* his or her sound, using what is effectively
a wooden box and making it vibrate in tune. All this
requires physical strength, as well as dexterity and control; a pianist, by contrast, needs only to strike the cor-
rect piece of ivory and the note will issue forth. That's
a large "only," of course, and performers such as Claudio Arrau, Vladimir Horowitz, Rudolf Serkin, and
Arthur Rubinstein—to name a few great pianists who
played impeccably in their eighties and nineties—did
much more than touch the right key. But no stringed

instrumentalist of whom I'm aware performed to undiminished effect once muscularity gave out. They might engage in a "star turn" or form part of an ensemble, but the solo career of a violinist or cellist, like that of a dancer or athlete, is at some point foredoomed to shut down. (And this presumes full health; there are any number of muscular or neurological conditions that can afflict the player, forcing an early retirement.) I heard Casals on the cello at ninety, and what one admired was not the performance as such.

In his particular case, moreover, the silence had been self-imposed. During what might otherwise have been the high-water mark of his interpretative career, he simply abandoned the stage. Casals fled Franco's rule and refused all invitations, spending long years in the village of Prades in the French Pyrenees—chosen in part for its proximity to Spain, and where Catalan still can be read on signposts and heard in the cafés. There's a folk image of the aging cellist striding through the snow-filled pass, his instrument strapped to his back; in fact he and his entourage boarded a train in Bordeaux. And one should not romanticize his Villa Collette on the outskirts of Prades or the church of San Miguel de Cuxa on the slopes of Mount Canigou; the times were hard, fare lean. In that small town where he lived in exile (and the ancient monastery where Casals performed the six Bach suites) there's neither *luxe* nor *volupté*, though *calme* would have pertained. The landscape of Cuxa is unforgiving; in the garden of the monastery (founded 878 A.D.) the saint who hallowed it by sleeping on the stony ground has his outline incised in the rock. Dust, olives, police scrutiny, silence: These would have been the cellist's daily portion, not caviar and applause.

For Pablo Casals, however, artistic integrity was an ingrained mode of behavior, and his fierce refusal to accommodate to Fascism felt all encompassing. He wrote; he studied; he taught a few students and occupied himself with the Spanish Republican cause. In many ways the wealthy and much-traveled virtuoso transformed himself in that decade from an outward-facing to an inward-focused musician. He gave only a very few concerts in the 1940s, and the bulk of his recordings date from 1950 on, by which time he was already well into his seventies and had lost full force if not expressiveness. As teacher and impresario he retained the sort of power that no longer emerged while he played. In the final phase of his career he moved from performing on the cello to composing and conducting, and in this manner could contrive to keep on keeping on.[9]

> I was born with an ability, with music in me, that is all. No special credit was due me. The only credit we claim is for the use we make of the talent we are given. That is why I urge young musicians: Don't

be vain because you happen to have talent. You are not responsible for it; it was not of your doing. What you do with your talent is what matters. You must cherish this gift. Do not demean or waste what you have been given. Work—work constantly and nourish it.

Further:[10]

Work helps prevent one from getting old. I, for one, cannot dream of retiring. Not now or ever. Retire? The word is alien and the idea inconceivable to me. I don't believe in retirement for anyone in my type of work, not while the spirit remains. My work is my life. I cannot think of one without the other. To retire means to begin to die. The man who works and is never bored is never old. Work and interest are the best remedy for age. Each day I am reborn. Each day I must begin again.

Those last two statements seem germane; "reborn," he started again with a relation to music that did not depend on concertizing or a solo instrument. Rehearsal and instruction offered both "work and interest," and he was "never bored." This may well be an essential component of productive vitality in old age; for someone who claims that "to retire means to begin to die," a certain kind of lastingness proves as natural and indispensable as breath.

The Marlboro Music Festival, in Marlboro, Vermont, is a family affair, and Casals participated in that festival for years. They eat, sleep, drink, and argue music there, with an informal earnestness that marries practice to performance—the apprentice and the master craftsman side by side. On July 11, 1970, I watched Casals conducting Beethoven's Egmont Overture in the music barn at Marlboro; the Maestro was bent and infirm. In conversation he seemed weary, abstracted, and those who attended him shook their heads; he had not been well. It took him minutes to walk from the wings, inching laboriously forward, taking small uncertain steps to the podium and hauling himself up into position as if every movement was painful and might just prove his last.

The orchestra waited, respectful, while he regained his spent breath. The silence extended, expanded; the Maestro stared down at his feet. Never large, he appeared to have shrunk. We worried, we asked each other, *sotto voce,* if he required assistance and should be helped from the stage.

And then, of a sudden, Casals raised both arms and was transformed. He threw himself forward, exhorting the players, galvanic, increasing the tempo, wielding the baton as though it were weightless and conducting the

Egmont at speed. He showed the *brio* and athletic exuberance of men not half his age. The *fortissimi* thundered, the barn fairly rocked, the celebration of freedom over oppression with which the overture (and Goethe's play) ends was just as sounding and resounding as Beethoven might have dreamed it in June of 1810.

When the last note died down, the conductor's arms dropped. He bent his bald head. Again, he looked old and exhausted; again he took slow weary steps and shuffled off into the wings while the hall full of people applauded. All his energy had gone into the music; there was, it appeared, nothing left.

• • •

Friedrich Hölderlin may have imagined renown in the carpenter's house, believing "Scardanelli's" reams of poetry would be read. Many of those fragments are in fact extant; others have been lost. But only the most assiduous of his admirers study what he wrote in Tübingen, and by and large the private work stays private. Pablo Casals commenced each morning with a form of devotional observance, playing, on piano or cello, a passage from the Bach Suites; he did not, however, expect that performance to be heard or recorded. The writer and the cellist each withdrew.

So too did Claude Monet. If Hölderlin continued to write, to no discernible effect, and Casals changed the mode of his public performance, there's a third type of creative engagement at life's end. And here the *quality* of art produced becomes a crucial issue. The work of the old poet seems empty, uninspired; the work of the old musician had little to do with the cello, and his achievement shifted ground. But the final project of the painter—the water-lily series known as the *Nymphéas*—is thought by many critics to have been his best.

As Rudolf Arnheim expresses it, in his seminal essay "On the Late Style":[11]

> In Monet's last landscapes we see the final outcome of a lifelong development, during which the subject matter was gradually absorbed by an ever more conspicuous texture, fully realized in his water lilies, his footbridge paintings, and other late works. Essential to our appreciation of these works, however, is the fact that, despite the radical transformation of the subject matter, all the fullness and wealth of experienced reality remains present. The greatest possible range of artistic content reaches from the concreteness of the individual things of nature to the uniformity of the artist's all-encompassing view.

Born in 1840, Monet died in 1926, and only in the final months, when entirely enfeebled, did he cease painting. One of the six founders of Impressionism as an artistic movement, he had a long embattled history (of exclusion from juried exhibitions, then inclusion in the vanguard and acceptance by collectors). The slow shift in status from outsider to elder statesman describes the arc of a career that's not so much an arc as a straight upward trajectory. Less and less did he care for commercial success, staying home in Giverny, a village on the River Seine, forty miles northwest of Paris. By preference Monet showed pictures only to his dealer, Paul Durand-Ruel, and a trusted circle of friends; at the last, one has the sense he painted for himself, and himself alone. As early as April 27, 1907, he wrote Durand-Ruel:[12]

> I'm very dissatisfied with myself, but that's better than producing things that are mediocre. I'm not postponing this show because I want to exhibit as many pictures as possible. On the contrary, I feel I have too few works worthy of being shown to the public. I have five or six at most that merit consideration, and have just, to my great satisfaction, destroyed at least thirty.... As time goes by I recognize those pictures that are good and those that should not be kept.

The paintings "that merit consideration" remain; they are objects preserved while a morning cadenza or scrap of rhymed verse disappears. Imagine for a moment what would happen to the record of Impressionism if the work of this artist's old age had been nonselectively destroyed. A canvas is an artifact that can outlive its maker, and the hundreds of thousands of visitors who now stand rapt in front of his water lilies would have astonished Monet; he labored in a privacy that grew near absolute.

Some of this had to do with his horror of the First World War, the catastrophic conditions abroad. Some had to do with deteriorating health, in particular his rheumatism and the cataracts that afflicted his sight. (As with Edgar Degas, whose eyes failed, or Pierre-Auguste Renoir, whose arthritis required he wedge the paintbrush between his fingers, the physical decline of Claude Monet had pictorial ramifications; his outlines grew less definite, his colors more pronounced.) One of the ways an aging artist comes to terms with physical change—as suggested by Casals—is to shift the locus of endeavor, and the painter narrowed focus to the point of near obsession. When young he had painted in all sorts of weather; now he no longer felt compelled to work outside. Increasingly reluctant to leave the house in Giverny, and solvent enough to maintain the establishment (he employed six gardeners), Monet fashioned a sequence of oils exponentially more numerous than the series of bridges or poplars or grain stacks or cathedrals he had already produced. Before, he had traveled to locate his subjects; now canvas after canvas reported on home ground.

In this regard, his "final" period is a function of geography: the farmhouse and its teeming garden in the town of Giverny. Monet afforded to his flowerbeds the kind of close attention he had earlier paid railway stations or rivers in winter or outcroppings of rock—with the important distinction that all these preexisted his attempt to capture any "impression" they made. The cities of London and Venice, it goes without saying, did not require his pictorial rendition in order to be viewed. In his farmhouse, however, he was both principal witness and maker; the lily pond was his to shape, the garden and Japanese bridges to build. And if his vision now was less than twenty-twenty, what he trained himself to paint had an inward-facing coherence that outstripped mere accuracy; his final efforts prefigure abstraction, making clinical exactness seem beside the point.

The aesthetic of "Impressionism" must have helped him here. The notion, for example, of the shifting play of light (as opposed to unaltered illumination) would have enabled the old artist to rely on what he saw while looking—this even when his eyesight had gone dim. As he told the American painter Lilla Cabot, "When you go out to paint, try to forget what objects you have before you, a tree, a house, a field."[13] The pictures of the *Nymphéas* take advantage of the wavering imprecision an oculist might hope to mend, so that *vision*—in its secondary meaning—may make luminous a blurry scumbled scene.

The poet Lisel Mueller has captured all this brilliantly, in "Monet Refuses the Operation." As of 1919, the painter was urged (among others, by his friend Georges Clemenceau) to have the cataracts attended to; in 1923 he had operations on his right eye, and glasses improved his eyesight—but only briefly, fitfully, and he had trouble distinguishing color. Mueller's poem begins:[14]

> Doctor, you say there are no haloes
> around the streetlights in Paris
> and what I see is an aberration
> caused by old age, an affliction.
> I tell you it has taken me all my life
> to arrive at the vision of gas lamps as angels,
> to soften and blur and finally banish
> the edges you regret I don't see,
> to learn that the line I called the horizon
> does not exist and sky and water,
> so long apart, are the same state of being....

If Hölderlin's tower attests to vacancy—few visitors, scant furniture—the house in Giverny is now a site of pilgrimage, replete with school groups and tour groups and multilingual guides. Monet's collection of Japanese prints festoons the walls; the dining room table has cut flowers on it, and the chairs in his large studio seem ready to be occupied, as once they were in family photographs everywhere out on display. The gift shop (postcards, posters, calendars, kitchen implements, scarves) constitutes a literal cottage industry, and the artist's *retraite* has grown populous in the extreme. Those crowds who walk the garden paths provide a startling addition to what the painter painted; none of his final land- or waterscapes have people central to them. After 1886 he dispensed entirely with the human form. Humanity's intrusion into nature is figured forth as bridge or rowboat or by a bright parasol in the middle distance. Yet in the Musée d'Orsay or the Musée Marmottan or MOMA and at "blockbuster" exhibitions everywhere, paying customers pay homage to the man who excised them in favor of flowers and light.[15]

I had always, since my sixtieth year, contemplated making a synthesis of each of the categories of subjects to which I had devoted my attention; a synthesis in which I would combine my former impressions and perceptions in one picture, or sometimes in two.... I waited until the idea had taken shape, until the arrangement and composition of the motifs had gradually inscribed itself on my brain....

The project of the *Nymphéas* extended for decades. Monet rented the Giverny house in 1883 and purchased it seven years later; in 1893 he added the pond. His first painting of a water lily came as early as 1895; thirty years thereafter, he remained in thrall to his patterned waterscape, as well as the wisteria above his bridge, and irises. Voltaire's life-tenet, "Cultivate your garden," found a disciple in this painter, and it's important to remember the seasonal aspect of growth and decay— the rhythms, as it were, of youth and maturation and old age. From the outset he envisioned his water lilies as a series; more than 250 are extant, and he planned them to be mounted together as a kind of interior decoration. This ambition was realized after his death, when a selection of linked canvases was installed in the Musée de l'Orangerie (with Prime Minister Clemenceau's sponsorship) in 1927.

One needn't glamorize the sanctity and focused commitment of a pair of artists such as Casals and Monet; both were canny managers of their own careers. Ego entered in enormously, and a competitive jostling for position; Monet was negotiating with collectors and the French government, driving up the prices of his paintings, until the very end. Both men were fierce and stubborn as well as self-absorbed and prone to fits of prideful temper; it's not an accident that their influence persisted in old age. At a certain point, retirement may prove a useful strategy, and this is particularly true in our celebrity culture; Howard Hughes and Greta Garbo, to take two examples, grew more compelling to the public once they became reclusive. I'm not suggesting the cellist or the painter *planned* the final stages of their artistic reputation; only that they accepted and profited from the admiration of the young.

Auguste Rodin, it's said, scattered marble chips and powder on his hair when a rich patron came to call, emerging from his studio distracted-seeming and wielding a chisel so as to give the impression of just having been interrupted in his morning's work. And the bantam pipe-smoking cellist, with his much younger and beautiful wife, or the white-bearded patriarch at his farmhouse table, routinely welcomed those who came to pay respects. "None are so old as those who have outlived enthusiasm"—so wrote Henry David Thoreau. Both cellist and painter did continue as enthusiasts, and they conveyed this to visitors; it was a component of their status at the end. The word itself derives from the Greek *en theos,* and signals the arrival of the penetrating god.

What interests me in this third case is how Monet took advantage of what might have seemed a deficit, how he incorporated loss into artistic gain. The photographs of the painter in old age (looking rather like Rodin, another titan of creative industry) suggest a physical robustness that goes some distance to explaining his unstoppable output at Giverny. This was his great undertaking and, like Michelangelo's labor on the Sistine Ceiling, an act of sustained concentration. Rheumatic and more than half blind, in mourning for such friends as Stéphane Mallarmé and Alfred Sisley as well as a number of family members, Monet nonetheless continued to paint—by his own attestation from seven to eleven each morning and then again all afternoon—producing a kind of pantheist chapel and shrine to the visible world.

CHAPTER FIVE

"My Muse Is Young"

I was good looking once like that young man, but
my unpractised verse was full of infirmity, my Muse
old as it were, and now I am old and rheumatic and
nothing to look at, but my Muse is young.

William Butler Yeats, "The Bounty of Sweden,"
Nobel Prize Acceptance Speech

The reader will have noticed that most of my subjects are male. In part, no doubt, this mirrors my
own gender and those models I have taken over
time. More to the point, perhaps, it's simple statistical
fact that the great bulk of recognized artists in our culture's history were men. Anonymity has shrouded the
creative achievements of women, and such glittering

examples as Marie de France or Lady Murasaki were the exception not rule. For every Artemisia Gentileschi, Hildegard von Bingen, or Aphra Behn we know the names of a dozen male painters, composers, and writers. George Eliot disguised her sex with her publishing *nom de plume,* and we can only guess how many others— witness Virginia Woolf's invention of Shakespeare's lost gifted sister—had their talents undervalued or their labor blocked.

The inequity of this has been addressed by scholars and critics increasingly; an imbalance is being redressed. In orchestras and galleries and bookstores, women thrive. A career in art seems more and more available today to female practitioners, and—as with the academy—the playing field grows level and the players gender blind. But it remains the case that prurient interest in the private lives of women has as much to do with their public profile as does the work itself. Camille Claudel is celebrated as Rodin's unhappy mistress as well as for her achievement as sculptor; Frida Kahlo first garnered attention as the wife of Diego Rivera. Vanessa Bell, Helen Frankenthaler, Lee Krasner, Louise Nevelson, Nikki de Saint Phalle, and the rest are known at least in part because of their romantic attachments, and though such painters as Picasso and Pascin were understood to be inveterate womanizers it somehow has been taken as a detail of biography and not a salient feature of the work.

No artist has been scrutinized more closely in this regard than was Georgia O'Keeffe. Born in 1887 in Sun Prairie, Wisconsin, she died just short of a century later, at the age of ninety-eight, in her beloved Santa Fe, New Mexico. Arguably the most famous female painter of the American twentieth century, her career is inextricably associated with that of Alfred Stieglitz, her lover and sponsor as well as creative adviser in the early years. Their courtship and collaboration and marriage and ensuing separation are the stuff of gossip if not legend; Stieglitz's photographs of Georgia O'Keeffe did much to establish her presence in the world of art. Between 1918 and 1937 he printed more than three hundred photos, and the erotic youthful nudes somehow presage later portraits of the old woman in retreat. Such men as Ansel Adams, Cecil Beaton, Philippe Halsman, Arnold Newman, Eliot Porter, Todd Webb, and Bruce Weber continued to take photographs, making a kind of collective icon of the austere aging face. In her final years, the desert solitary was accompanied by a young male employee, the potter and sculptor Juan Hamilton, to whom she willed many paintings and much of her estate.

That I begin my discussion of this creative artist in terms of the men in her life should demonstrate this chapter's first point; hers is not an achievement *in vacuo* but context, and the context counts. From an ambitious art student in Chicago and New York to an accomplished painter in Stieglitz's family home on Lake George to a seer invaded by white desert light, O'Keeffe has come to represent the very essence of "lastingness." Her paintings of flowers and skulls stripped to their bloom and bone fetch millions of dollars at auction, and the countryside she memorialized—much like Monet's at Giverny—now teems with tourists come to admire what she painted as a vacancy. There's a museum devoted to her work in Santa Fe, and the wait list for admission to her home in nearby Abiquiu is long.

Retreat implies withdrawal, and O'Keeffe's move to New Mexico had something of withdrawal in it; she left behind the art scene in Manhattan with an almost audible sigh of relief. She had spent time in Bermuda, Hawaii, and other "picturesque" places, but the inner and outer landscape she limned while in New Mexico approached true congruence. In *The Poetics of Space,* Gaston Bachelard (1884–1962) suggests that each of us prefers a particular vista, and there's no point to a hierarchical ranking of, say, a meadow or mountain, a forest or dell. The ocean is neither more nor less intrinsically beautiful than is a river or shoreline or waterfall or lake. Rather, what we all must do is seek out the surrounding space to which we most deeply respond, and this particular artist reacted to the American Southwest as though to revelation. From her first visit, in 1917, and the next in 1929, and then again, on an annual basis, until 1949 when she moved to New Mexico permanently, she had what might be called a conversion experience: This was and would be her landscape, and she knew it on the spot.

When O'Keeffe later remembered her first sight of Rancho de los Burros, with its views of ancient cliffs, she said, "As soon as I saw it, I knew I must have it. I can't understand people who want something badly but don't grab for it. I grabbed."[1] And her devotion endured. "Living out there has just meant happiness," she declared, at eighty-four. "Sometimes I think I'm half mad with love for this place."[2] Further, "When I think of death, I only regret that I will not be able to see this beautiful country anymore...unless the Indians are right and my spirit will walk here after I'm gone."[3]

Her spirit still does walk. The landscape itself appears unchanged—as does the house, with its adobe walls and clean-swept floors, its garden tools and elk skull, its Tiffany glasses and stereo system with which she might listen to music. The piled stones on the patio evoke a ghostly tenant; so do the herbs and stucco arches and black door and white bed. When you look at what she looked at here, the vivid clarity of O'Keeffe's pictorial rendering feels more like a function of realism than interpretative mannerism. As with the sunflowers of Van Gogh or the sunsets of Turner, the thing shown is a direct equivalent of the landscape seen.

What "might have been" is always problematic, and it's hard to know what her reputation would consist of had she never seen or painted the American Southwest. The cityscapes and studies of Lake George do of course merit attention, as do the rare portraits of such friends as Beauford Delaney. Her series of paintings of flowers were undertaken in New York, and the habit of abstraction was with her from the start. Indeed, her early abstract oils are among the first and best produced in America, and she was a gifted draughtsman all along. But one can't escape the sense that this painter made a qualitative leap when she discovered the "poetics" of surrounding space. The clarity of light and line, the sunbursts of color, the pictorial emblems of sex and death, *eros* as well as *thanatos*: All these signal O'Keeffe at both her most emphatic and suggestive. The spirit of place staked its claim. A major artist in maturity, she settled in New Mexico and pursued her original vision, working—by and large—alone.

In 1962, in her mid-seventies she offered this self-assessment to the writer Lee Nordness:[4]

> One works because I suppose it is the most interesting thing one knows how to do. The days one works are the best days. On the other days one is hurrying through the other things one imagines one has to do to keep one's life going. You get the garden planted. You

get the roof fixed. You take the dog to the vet. You spend a day with a friend. You learn to make a new kind of bread. You hunt up photographs for someone who thinks he needs them. You certainly have to do the shopping. You may even enjoy doing such things. You think they have to be done. You even think you have to have some visitors or take a trip to keep from getting queer living alone with just two chows. But always you are hurrying through these things with a certain amount of aggravation so that you can get at the paintings again because that is the high spot—in a way it is what you do all the other things for.... The painting is like a thread that runs through all the reasons for all the other things that make one's life.

That thread was thickly braided, and "the most interesting thing," even in the fallow periods, or those of nervous collapse. Here are a pair of much earlier letters to Stieglitz, the first dated July 29, 1937:[5]

Thursday afternoon—about 5—...I've been painting an old dead cedar against those purple hills I've painted so often. It is a tree that I made a drawing of long ago when I first came up here—I've been working on it yesterday and today—it looks promising. It's one of those things I've had in my so-called mind for a long time....

On August 16:[6]

Good Sunday morning to you!...I think I am through with my tree—it is the first thing I have done that when I stand it by the window and look at it—then I look out the window—it looks like what I see out the window, though it was painted a mile away. I think it really looks like here. Even at that I don't think it very good—I'll do it again.

The brilliant light, the signature paintings of crosses and skulls, of cliffs and clouds and half-closed doors, the very essence of her art in all its chill assertiveness and unblinking rigor: These images arose in Santa Fe and flourished there. Her earlier paintings of flowers and fruit were, in effect, microscopic, by which I mean closely focused, even magnified, and largely noncontextual: They fill the canvas full. The compositions in New Mexico, however, seem by contrast *telescopic,* powered by the middle distance or the distant view.

As had been the case for Claude Monet, the human figure disappeared, and O'Keeffe concentrated on landscape. With a few exceptions of birds in flight over Palo Duro Canyon or the hills of New Mexico, her canvases contained no living—or at least no nonvegetal—things. Increasingly she traveled, visiting Europe and the Far East, but the "vision" stayed rooted at home. Whereas

Titian in his great old age and Rembrandt in his final years grew more and more attentive to personality in portraiture, O'Keeffe became *im*-personal. "I have sat for so many artists that I would never ask anyone to do the same for me," she said. "I've always believed that I can get all that into a picture by suggestion. I mean the life that has been lived in a place."[7]

As with any such aesthetic there are dangers in rigidity, and it would stretch the truth to claim that her last paintings are her best. Although both fame and solitude increased during her life's long closing act, the painter came—or so I think—to substitute gesture for substance, to reject and not remain available to change. She had always had a tendency to strike an attitude if not a pose, and more and more the figure of O'Keeffe as desert prophet became synonymous with her stance as artist; the flowers and the fruits she'd drawn with anatomical exactness grew dessicate, not fecund, and color leached away. O'Keeffe had been proud of her eyesight as well as independence, and there's something doubly sad, though no doubt in person comforting, about the notion of Juan Hamilton helping her assess a piece of sculpture by running her hands across it so that she might "see." She was still at work in her nineties, increasingly committed to abstraction, but the years did take their toll, and the blind lame visionary who scrawled her signature on codicils leaving more and more to Hamilton was no longer self-sufficient. *Black Rock with Blue Sky and White Clouds,* painted in 1972 before she lost her eyesight, is one of the last completed oils and rife with the old mystery. Yet what it portends is unclear.

• • •

When William Butler Yeats, in "Among School Children," calls himself "A sixty-year-old smiling public man,"[8] he does so with a sense of role-playing displacement that verges on despair. Art is a privacy made public, not the other way around. The old, much-honored poet surrounded by lithe children can't bring himself to acknowledge how confounded by physical yearning he feels—but then he writes a poem (in the justified hope that thousands will read it) confessing to just such desire.

This is a constant concern in Yeats, particularly as he ages; in the "Crazy Jane" series or such ballads as "The Wild Old Wicked Man" he rails against the "bodily decrepitude" he describes with such precision. "Sick with desire, and fastened to a dying animal," the poet ruminates upon the paradox of being "out of nature" yet making it his subject. Poem after poem aspires to the oxymoronic condition of being "cold and passionate as the dawn," and Yeats's great achievement has to do with the sequential triad of "what is past, or passing, or to come." No artist of the twentieth century wrote more tellingly of transience or transformed it more persuasively into lines that last.

He began, of course, as a romantic, an adept of dream-powered yearning. The essence of such lyrics as "The Song of Wandering Aengus" or "The Lake Isle of Innisfree" is an attempt to seize the passing moment and gainsay Shakespeare's warning: "Youth's a stuff will not endure." Earlier, such forward-facing lines as "When you are old and grey and full of sleep..." predict a kind of constancy, the boastful insistence of passionate youth that passion *will* endure. His heroes of mythology and folklore, his figures of the countryside or wishing for "the cloths of heaven" all share the same conviction and propound the same ideal. The early Yeats seems almost a stereotype of the poet as romantic, and had he died or ceased to write by the age of forty he would be a minor figure in the history of verse.

Instead, he towers proudly over what he called the "singing school" and proffers instance after instance of "unageing intellect." That "paltry thing" and "coat upon a stick" becomes much more than scarecrow once taught to "clap its hands and sing, and louder sing." The verse plays and narratives and political poems and ballads each embody his final instruction: "Irish poets, learn your trade, / Sing whatever is well made." Technical agility goes hand-in-hand with conceptual fervor, and Yeats never loses or cheapens his desire to "articulate sweet sounds together." (I have conflated here, in order, phrases from "Sailing to Byzantium" and "Under Ben Bulben" and "Adam's Curse" so as to stress continuity, a sameness within change.) The first line of "Sailing to Byzantium" states, bitterly, of Ireland, "That is no country for old men." Yet he remained an Irish patriot until his death in 1939, at the age of seventy-three.

Sixteen years earlier, the poet had been awarded the Nobel Prize for Literature: a capstone of any career. He was informed of the honor, by telephone, between ten and eleven o'clock on a November night in Dublin, in 1923. Touchingly, as he records in his autobiography, he and his wife searched for a bottle of wine in the cellar but found nothing; then, "as a celebration is necessary we cook sausages."[9] This is a far cry indeed from the image of writer as noble carouser or exalted visionary; no matter how grand his position, the table stayed spartan at home.

Too, Yeats is generally considered to be one of the few writers whose major achievements came *after* that prize; such subsequent collections as *The Tower* (1928) and *The Winding Stair and Other Poems* (1933) contain many of his most celebrated poems. He was writing near the very end, composing his own epitaph, in "Under Ben Bulben," with "a cold eye." His is, in short, an unequivocal instance of that achievement in old age I posited at study's start as the test of lastingness; no catalog of men and women who enlarged their art in later life could fail to list his name.

How did he do it, we are entitled to wonder; what combination of good luck and rigor enabled this pattern of growth? His wacky theories and automatic writing and dose of monkey glands notwithstanding, William Butler Yeats exemplifies the figure of the artist working at or near the top of his bent in his last years. The moonstruck swain of Maud Gonne and Lady Gregory, the poetasting devotee of Madame Blavatsky and Cuchulain managed to emerge intact from some refiner's fire and, "once out of nature," sang with "passionate intensity" (again a conflation of "Sailing to Byzantium" and "The Second Coming"). Although he laments, in the latter poem, that "the best lack all conviction," he never lost his certainty that poetry must matter and its practice count.

The first fourteen lines of "Adam's Curse" (1902) comprise a kind of sonnet and state both the problem and case:[10]

> We sat together at one summer's end
> That beautiful mild woman, your close friend
> And you and I, and talked of poetry.
> I said: "a line will take us hours maybe;
> Yet if it does not seem a moment's thought
> Our stitching and unstitching has been naught.

Better go down upon your marrow bones
And scrub a kitchen pavement or break stones
Like an old pauper in all kinds of weather;
For to articulate sweet sounds together
Is to work harder than all these and yet
Be thought an idler by the noisy set
Of bankers, schoolmasters, and clergymen
The martyrs call the world."

We have one surviving recording of the poet performing his work. A series of tapes were produced by the BBC but lost to fire in World War II; some few minutes have been preserved. Yeats's singsong renderings of "The Lake Isle of Innisfree" and "The Song of the Old Mother" feel incantatory, nearly, and his pleasure in rhythm and rhyme is unmistakable. In this 1932 recording session the Laureate declares, "It gave me a devil of a lot of trouble to get into verse the poems that I am going to read, and that is why I will *not* read them as if they were prose." Sounding very much the Irish senator as well as bard, he recites his language lingeringly, emphasizing by example that the poet must "work harder than all these...bankers, schoolmasters, and clergymen" who constitute "the world."

His manuscripts attest to this. Painstaking, constantly rephrased, Yeats's variora show both his native fluency and habit of revision. By and large that close reworking comes in the service of simplicity—not, as with the prose of James Joyce, incremental and associative complexity. To pick another countryman whose topic is old age and its indignities, the elder Yeats predicts the aging Samuel Beckett: Renunciation is his subject, and acquiescence its yield. The woman blowing on the coals in "The Song of the Old Mother" is an emblem of the artist who "must work because I am old, / And the seed of the fire gets feeble and cold." But that poem appeared in *The Wind Among the Reeds* as early on as 1899, and is surrounded by lyrical praise of the young man's inamorata, her "passion-dimmed eyes and long heavy hair / That was shaken out over my breast" (from "He Reproves the Curlew"). The words "Lover" or "His beloved" appear in no fewer than a dozen of that volume's titles, and when "He Bids His Beloved Be at Peace" or "He Gives His Beloved Certain Rhymes" or "He Thinks of Those Who Have Spoken Evil of His Beloved," he does so with the fervor of besotted youth.

Things are very different by the time of the *Last Poems* (1936–1939). In the bitter, self-reflexive "Why Should Not Old Men Be Mad?" the poet closes with this assertion:

> ...No single story would they find
> Of an unbroken happy mind,
> A finish worthy of the start.

Young men know nothing of this sort,
Observant old men know it well;
And when they know what old books tell,
And that no better can be had,
Know why an old man should be mad.

And, in the triumphal "Lapis Lazuli," the last stanza closely examines an enduring work of art:

Every discoloration of the stone,
Every accidental crack or dent,
Seems a water-course or an avalanche,
Or lofty slope where it still snows
Though doubtless plum or cherry-branch
Sweetens the little half-way house
Those Chinamen climb towards, and I
Delight to imagine them seated there;
There, on the mountain and the sky,
On all the tragic scene they stare.
One asks for mournful melodies;
Accomplished fingers begin to play.
Their eyes mid many wrinkles, their eyes,
Their ancient, glittering eyes, are gay.

I know no more exact or exacting description of that which one might "delight to imagine" and the accomplishment of lastingness. The two final lines, with the thrice-iterated evocation of "their eyes" (and the sono-rous association with both "Ayes" and "I's") describe and celebrate and engender gaiety. The scene may well be "tragic" and the melodies are "mournful," but its seated witnesses are gay.

Previously, in *A Vision* (1925), he had espoused this notion of a self-effacing impersonality, and the fusion of the arts:[11]

> I think that in early Byzantium...religious, aesthetic and practical life were one, that architect and artificers— though not, it may be, poets, for language had been the instrument of controversy and must have grown abstract—spoke to the multitude and the few alike. The painter, the mosaic worker, the worker in gold and silver, the illuminator of sacred books, were almost impersonal, almost perhaps without the consciousness of individual design, absorbed in their subject-matter and that the vision of a whole people. They could copy out of old Gospel books those pictures that seemed as sacred as the text, and yet weave all into a vast design, the work of many that seemed the work of one, that made building, picture, pattern, metal-work of rail and lamp, seem but a single image....

This ideal of artistry that speaks "to the multitude and the few alike" requires concrete implementation, and

Yeats eschews abstraction on the poet's part. When he writes "the elemental creatures go / About my table, to and fro…" the context is domestic, and no matter what "vast image" troubles his imagination he yokes it to the writing desk and claims it is "…at hand." Further, and importantly, the maker's presence is anonymous; no names attach to the "painter, the mosaic worker…the illuminator" who labor "without the consciousness of individual design." That "almost impersonal" ambition—to be an instrument of artistic transmission and not, as its creator, singled out—stayed with him till the end.

This is, I think, a crucial component of the final years. As early on as 1914, when he published "A Coat" in *Responsibilities,* he disavowed "embroideries / Out of old mythologies" and claimed "Song, let them take it / For there's more enterprise / In walking naked." A quarter of a century later, in "The Circus Animals' Desertion," the writer is explicit about the condition of "being but a broken man"—his lack of interest when old in "Lion and woman and the Lord knows what…" If, in "A Coat," Yeats willingly renounces the apparatus of display, by the time of the *Last Poems,* he can find no alternative:

> I sought a theme and sought for it in vain,
> I sought it daily for six weeks or so.
> Maybe at last, being but a broken man,

> I must be satisfied with my heart, although
> Winter and summer till old age began
> My circus animals were all on show. . . .

This attestation of exhaustion has its own yield, finally; after the poet makes a survey of "old themes," listing previous subjects and preoccupations, he ends with the assertive couplet: "I must lie down where all the ladders start / In the foul rag-and-bone shop of the heart." It's one of the great dividends of art, and one Yeats manages greatly, that the very act of naming absence makes of it a presence: By such a conjuration, the writer can trick time.

• • •

Franz Liszt completes this chapter's trio: also honored in old age, also working in a kind of willed retreat. From a virtuoso gaped at and applauded by thousands—the matinee-idol incarnate, the essence of celebrity both as pianist and composer—he became the austere Abbé Liszt. This was never a total reversal; Liszt denied himself few comforts, having received the tonsure, and had earlier composed his *Consolations* and the first volumes of *Années de Pelèrinage* while luxuriating in Fontainebleau or on the shores of Lake Como. Turn by turn he seems an ascetic or a romantic aesthete. Faith and musicianship sustain each other in the act of worship, and few composers in the Western canon—from Palestrina and Bach through Fauré and Bloch—so entirely embody the marriage of spirit and flesh.

Yet it was a warring marriage, and the tension is hard to ignore. No rock star of the present day is more adored than was this artist, no ticket now more coveted than the chance to hear him concertizing then. Women fainted or threw themselves at him; aristocrats begged for an audience and potentates showered their praise. His name was omnipresent and his influence proved vast. Hailed as the legatee of Beethoven and the precursor (as well as father-in-law and sponsor) of Richard Wagner, routinely compared to Mozart and Chopin, Liszt's position in the pantheon is fixed. Mostly we remember him as long-haired, wild-eyed, slender: a dazzling performer, whose feats of musical interpretation, improvisation, and endurance put present artists to shame.

But in his last years he accepted no fees, grown world-weary and enfeebled, choosing to celebrate the Mass rather than to be by masses celebrated. Eyewitness accounts of his early concerts have him flinging himself at the piano; later he sat like a stone. Perhaps the most accomplished pianist of his generation (even, there are those who argue, in the history of music), Liszt performed less and less often in public. And what he played was very different in old age. As Anthony Storr observes:[12]

Liszt...died in his seventy-fifth year. For about fifteen years before his death, his music shows a remarkable change. There is none of the old flamboyance,
and no more transcendental virtuosity—or at least
no virtuosity for its own sake. Instead, there is a pre-
occupation with Hungarian folksong; the genuine
peasant variety, not the *ersatz* kind to be found in the
early rhapsodies. There is also a partial abandonment
of conventional tonality, which anticipates Schoenberg and Bartók. Instead of using the habitual system
of stating a theme, developing it through various
keys, recapitulating it, and finally arriving at a goal,
Liszt experiments with violent contrasts and clashes,
and with impressionist effects achieved by the sus-
taining pedal.

Born in Raiding in the Kingdom of Hungary on
October 22, 1811, the composer died on July 31, 1886,
in Bayreuth. As had held true for Mozart and Felix Mendelssohn, Liszt's gifts were proclaimed early on. (Too,
as was the case with Mozart, his career would be pro-
pelled by his own father's musical ambition; Adam Liszt
opposed his son's desire to prepare for the priesthood
when young.) The years as a child prodigy began with
a debut in Vienna on the first day of December 1822,
where he played Hummel and Rossini as well as an
improvisation on the *Allegretto* of Beethoven's Seventh

Symphony. According to legend, Beethoven himself attended and kissed the boy, congratulating him. In fact Beethoven was elsewhere, and his presence but a product of the performer's imagination; his teacher that year had been Antonio Salieri, and he later studied with Ferdinando Paer. With Paer's help, Liszt composed the opera *Don Sanche, ou le Château de l'Amour*, which premiered on October 17, 1825, before he turned fifteen.

His ascent thereafter was rapid and his success enormous. In concerts all over Europe, the virtuoso was applauded and adored. From 1839 to 1847 Liszt traveled without respite, being everywhere received with excited adulation. The only comparable figure—though on another instrument—is the Italian violinist Niccolò Paganini (1782–1840), whose reputation and reception does prefigure Liszt's. But Paganini was widely rumored to have been possessed by the devil, with gifts conferred through some satanic compact; by contrast the Hungarian was celebrated for his inspirational presence and thought to be angelic in his art.

By the end of 1847, moreover, Liszt rejected all personal payment, concertizing instead for charity. He traveled to Budapest, Bayreuth, Paris, Vienna, Brussels, London, Rome; he "rusticated" in Bellagio or at the Villa d'Este. Though his *amours* and romantic entanglements were bruited early on, and though his early years were seldom free from scandal (with such partners as

Adèle de Laprunarède, Carolyne von Sayn-Wittgenstein, and Marie d'Agoult, by whom he had three children), his later reputation has to do with selflessness. Testimonials abound. His largesse was habitual, his charity widespread. He raised money to relieve those suffering at Peath from the inundation of the Danube in 1837, and when the grateful populace raised a statue in his honor, he insisted that the commission go to a youthful sculptor; in 1845 he helped erect the monument to Beethoven at Bonn.

In 1849 the composer settled in Weimar and made of that city, once again (as it had been in Goethe's time), a capital of culture. For a dozen years, as *Kapellmeister Extraordinaire,* he mounted operas—including the first performance of Wagner's *Lohengrin* in 1850—and choral works and those orchestral pieces on which his reputation now in important part rests. The yield of his sojourn in Weimar consists of this transition from virtuoso to composer; having relinquished the pianoforte in concert, Liszt turned from the keyboard to a desk. And what he thereafter composed has the feel of true modernity, sounding in its pruned severity more like contemporary music than the pyrotechnical extravagance of his years onstage. As the critic Humphrey Searle puts it:[13]

> The style has become extremely stark and austere, there are long passages in single notes and a considerable use of whole-tone chords, and anything

resembling a cadence is avoided; in fact, if a work does end with a common chord it is more often in an inversion than in root position. The result is a curiously indefinite feeling, as if Liszt was launching out into a new world of whose possibilities he was not quite sure. For the majority of these works he returned to his first love, the piano; but in general the old pianistic glitter is absent—Liszt was now writing for himself, and no longer for his public.

Every musical occasion must incorporate an audience, an awareness on the musician's part of what *can* be performed and how sound will be heard. The dynamic interaction of composer, performer, and audience is indispensable to music-making, and many if not all of the great composers were accomplished instrumentalists as well. His decades at the keyboard would have enabled Liszt to imagine auditors, and one senses in the final work a refusal to pander, a turning away from display. Some of this has to do with the passage of time, the slow transition from iconoclast to elder statesman; in this regard, no doubt, change was and is inevitable. Whereas the youthful Liszt displayed a boundless energy, toward the end he breathed and walked in pain. The years did take their toll. (Here it's tempting to draw parallels to Beethoven, whose incremental deafness fueled the strange sonorities and radical tonal departures of the late quartets. If nothing else, the hearing loss inevitable in old age will alter intonation; the loss of cilia within the ear may well be as important to the formulation of late style as is the failing eyesight of a painter or the physical enfeeblement a writer like Yeats mourns.) In the third volume of his capacious biography, Alan Walker reports:[14]

> On July 2, 1881, Liszt fell down the stairs of the Hofgärtnerei. It was his traumatic entry into old age. Not quite seventy years old, he had until then enjoyed reasonably good health, and his body had retained much of the slimness and suppleness of his youth. The accident changed all that.... From this episode Liszt's decline into the infirmities of old age can be traced. The accident seemed to trigger a number of ailments that until then had been lying dormant within him—including dropsy, asthma, insomnia, a cataract of the left eye, and chronic heart disease. This latter illness would kill him within five years.

He taught; he wrote; he met colleagues at home. He received a large number of students, tutoring them for free. The Abbé had made art his religion; now the reverse too held true. Gustav Schirmer, the founder of the great music publishing house, asked the master (who seemed melancholy) if religious faith did not help him as his end drew near. There's something disingenuous about Liszt's reply: "Here on earth I have been given the opportunity, and also the ability, to undertake a leading role in the service of Art, of artists, and of mankind itself. I now wonder again and again whether, after the great transition, I shall be able to continue to do so."[15]

"After the great transition..." seems a pious way to euphemize approaching death, and the idea that he might "undertake a leading role in the service of Art" from beyond the grave is—albeit true—disquieting. A whiff of sanctity did hover near Liszt's lodgings, and to some degree his *cénacle* partook of sanctimoniousness, a kind of enforced idolatry in those who came to call. But mostly it seems genuine, and the respect well earned. As Sacheverell Sitwell, in his quirky biography, *Liszt*, observes: "The unselfishness and the true humility of his life for the rest of his days are without parallel.... He lived contentedly upon some three or four hundred pounds a year, having no luxuries, drinking the cheapest and coarsest of wines; and even where his one weakness was concerned, in the matter of cigars, he would give away good ones that had been presented to him and smoke, for preference, the cheapest sorts that he could buy."[16]

This diminution over time is characteristic of the species; we eat, drink, fight, and copulate less riotously as we grow old. Nor *could* Liszt have continued at that furious opening pace. His sacred and his secular chorales, his organ music and orchestral transcriptions, his opera paraphrases and chamber works were produced in such abundance that it seems unavoidable there would be chaff as well as grain. (One has a similar reaction to Telemann and Vivaldi; the output is enormous and parts of it composed with less than full attentiveness or, as it were, by the left hand.) But in his old age Liszt, like Yeats, came to substitute efficiency for energy, and the music of his final years is shorn of ornamentation in a way that those who heard him early on would not likely have predicted.

In the end, moreover, he retained his allegiance to the concert stage in the very act of renouncing it; this is not so much a paradox as natural progression. His habit of revision and updating what he wrote is not in essence different from his earlier practice of improvisation; both yoke the idea of performance to that of composition. And though his personal history is inalienably romantic—his chiseled countenance, lean figure, his Abbé's cloak, his reputation as seducer—such an ambition is classical: The act of concertizing and the act of creation become one and the same. To make is to perform.

Here, in a letter to his English pupil Walter Bache, he gracefully declines the invitation to be his own interpreter:[17]

My very dear friend:

They seem determined in London to push me to the piano. I cannot allow this to happen in public, as my seventy-five-year-old fingers are no longer suited to it, and Bülow, Saint-Saëns, Rubinstein, and you, dear Bache, play my compositions much better than what is left of my humble self.

Perhaps it would be opportune if friend Hueffer would have the kindness to let the public know, by a short announcement, that Liszt only ventures to appear as a grateful visitor, and neither in London nor anywhere else as a man with an interest in his fingers.

In all friendship yours,

F. Liszt

Budapest

February 11, 1886

Liszt's final performance came on July 19, 1886. While traveling to Bayreuth, and prevailed upon to listen to a concert in the Casino of Luxembourg, he agreed to play his own first *Liebestraum*, one of his arrangements of Chopin's *Chants Polonais*, and the sixth of his *Soirées de Vienne*. "This was not only the last time that Liszt played in public, but it may also have been the last time that he ever touched the keys of a piano. With these three pieces…Liszt's magical playing fell silent for ever."[18]

Were it not for his own compositions, that silence would remain. His pianistic exploits are the stuff of legend and cannot be retrieved. The thunderous performances, the thunderous ovations, the feats of endurance and agility have been consigned to history. The comparison as virtuoso to Schumann, Thalberg, Rubinstein, and others, the sponsorship of Wagner, the influence on Strauss and Mahler: All these are components of celebrity and over time must fade.

But Franz Liszt created piano pieces (such as *Les Jeux d'Eaux à la Villa d'Este* or *Carillon* from *Weihnachstbaum*) and *Lieder* (such as his settings for poems by de Musset and Hugo) and the large-scale setting of a poem by Longfellow, *Die Glocken des Strassburger Münsters*, and the *Mephisto Waltzes* and *Nuages Gris* and *Unstern,* for successors to perform. These late works—too many to enumerate and too various to group together—in their ascetic purity are the absolute obverse of what he began with, and very fine music indeed. The third and final volume of the *Années de Pèlerinage,* completing a lifelong pilgrimage, records a goal attained.

The First Folio portrait of Shakespeare, known as the "Droeshout" and believed to be an authentic likeness of the aging playwright. (© Corbis)

The building now known as Hölderlin's Tower, in the town of Tübingen, in southern Germany. Mad, the poet spent the last half of his life overlooking the River Neckar. (Tourismus-Marketing GmbH Baden-Wüerttemberg)

Claude Monet in the farmhouse garden at Giverny, which he lovingly planted and painted. It was the central landscape of his final years. (© Corbis)

A contemporary photograph of the lily ponds in Giverny, the inspiration for the series of oil paintings known as the Nymphéas. (Marvin Parnes)

Hungarian composer and performer Franz Liszt in 1886, the year of his death at age seventy-five. (© Hulton Deutsch Collection/Corbis)

Count Lev Tolstoy in peasant's garb—a characteristic costume of his later years. (© Bettman/Corbis)

The Catalan virtuoso violoncellist Pablo (Pao) Casals, in an early publicity photo. (© Hulton Deutsch Collection/Corbis)

Casals with his student Bernard Greenhouse, outside the Villa Colette in the village of Prades in the French Pyrenees in 1946. (Charles Winkelstein, MD)

Bernard Greenhouse playing the cello at the age of ninety-four outside his home in Wellfleet, Massachusets. (Diane Asséo Griliches)

Georgia O'Keeffe at home in Abiquiu, New Mexico. Few artists have been more photographed, or their faces better known. (Photo by Philippe Halsman © Halsman Estate, University of Michigan Museum of Art, Gift of Dr. Seymour and Barbara Adelson)

William Butler Yeats as "a sixty-year-old (not so) smiling public man." (© Hulton Deutsch Collection/Corbis)

Alice Neel: Self-portrait, 1980. The artist is eighty years old. (National Portrait Gallery, Smithsonian Institution © Estate of Alice Neel, 1980)

Goya Attended by Dr. Arrieta, 1820. *The inscription reads: "Goya, thankful to his friend Arrieta: for the skill and care with which he saved his life during his short and dangerous illness, endured at the end of 1819, at seventy-three years of age. He painted it in 1820."* (The Minneapolis Institute of Arts)

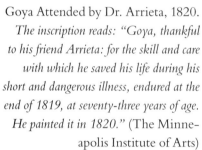

The Sleep of Reason Produces Monsters, *from Goya's series of etchings* Caprichos, 1799. (University of Michigan Museum of Art/Gift of Kurt Delbanco in honor of Nicholas Delbanco, and partial purchase with the funds from the W. Hawkins Ferry Fund)

Max Eastman and Nicholas Delbanco on Martha's Vineyard, 1967.
(Photo courtesy of www.PeterSimon.com)

John Updike and Nicholas Delbanco in Bennington, Vermont, 1980.
(Elena Delbanco)

The author and his father, Kurt Delbanco, standing in front of an oil by Willem de Kooning in 1994. (Elena Delbanco)

Clara Wieck Schumann and her husband, Robert, in the early days of their marriage, before his time in Endenich, the asylum where he died. (© Bettman/Corbis)

CHAPTER SIX

"If We Want Things to Stay as They Are..."

Neither the sun nor death can be looked at steadily.

François, Duc de la Rochefoucauld, Maxim 25

My mother loved the opera and tried to instill a similar devotion in her sons. In my case, it must be admitted, she had small success. I remember being disappointed when Don Giovanni took his final leap into the pit of hell and—leaning out over the balcony railing—I could see the stage hands catch him where he fell. An overweight Salome failed to excite me once she took off seven veils; she remained a thick aging lady in a body stocking and not the seductress I'd hoped to see dance. But *Aida* was a winner; we went on my thirteenth birthday to Rome's Baths of Caracalla. There were elephants in the triumphal parade, and neither a summer rain squall nor the great steaming gouts of elephant dung could dampen my enthusiasm for the spectacle involved. Giuseppe Verdi, it was clear, was a showman as well as a composer, and I can remember thinking, Wow, this stuff can be *fun*.

Otello is an opera I did come to admire. Fifteen by then, I studied it in music class, and knew the story and the characters from the English play. Too, I had begun to learn about love and feel the pangs of jealousy; I owned the recording with Mario del Monaco and, as Desdemona, Renata Tebaldi. Often, late at night, I'd play her piteous rendition of "The Willow Song" or the duet with which Act I concludes. As with any repeated exposure to excellence, the more I listened the more I learned, and "music appreciation" in this instance went beyond the question of whether or not the lovers would live happily ever after, exiting on a high C. Their intricate exchange of vows, the harp arpeggios and contrapuntal melody and soaring devotional rapture made what was secular sacred and transformed what was language to song.

Still later, newly married, I found myself in the north German town of Bremen, and with an unscheduled evening; my wife and I bought tickets to a local production of *Otello*. It was being performed, as it turned out, in German. Although the singers were accomplished and the opera company fully professional, I couldn't make the shift. In the back of my brain Tebaldi, sweetly yielding, took her brave soldier's arm at the end of their transcendent duet and followed him in to the marital bed; his line—a sustained seductive invitation—is *"Vien . . . Venere splende."* "Come, Venus is shining," he sings, and the cellos return and the curtain descends and lovers leave to applause.

In German, however, the *Heldentenor* who played the part of Othello had the unenviable task of singing, *"Komm. Venus erscheint."* He got the notes right, and the *sostenuto*, but to my ear there was something ineradicably wrong about the sound of it, with nothing the tenor could do. Together, he and his obedient *Frau* marched in lockstep off the stage.

So here was another such lesson: The composer and librettist must work in close tandem, and the sonorous Italian—as opposed to the guttural German—is a critical part of the whole. None of this is news, of course; each opera, when successful, employs a multiplicity of components in complementary unison; it's not an accident the word is the plural of *opus,* for this is plausibly the most synthetic art form of them all. Collaborative, too, in that each of the functional elements fuse, making the whole greater than the sum of parts. And Giuseppe

Verdi, I had come to understand, was a spectacular practitioner of the art my mother loved, preeminent at matching language to pure melody, the drama of tuneful romance.

His public knew this from the start; he was honored and applauded while he lived. And it was a very long life. Born on October 10, 1813, in Le Roncole, a village of a hundred peasants in the Duchy of Parma, he died in a unified Italy that could be crisscrossed by train. At his birth the mode of travel was on foot or by a horse-drawn coach; when he died the Fiat Corporation was already two years old. The infant Verdi inhabited a Europe at war with Napoleon Bonaparte; by the date of his death (January 27, 1901), the ideals of "liberty, equality, fraternity" were being espoused by socialists. The wars and uprisings and communes of 1830, 1848, and 1870 each had come and gone.

For most of that time he made music. There are stories, probably apocryphal, about his native and even prenatal talent: Musicians serenade his mother during pregnancy, she climbs a ringing bell tower to escape a Cossack raid, young Giuseppe is so enraptured by the organ he forgets to serve the host at Mass, he attacks a spinet with a hammer because he fails to find the chord of C minor, and so on and so forth. Whatever the truth of such stories, his gift was announced early on. By the time that he was ten years old, Verdi was the village organist and by his teens composing piano pieces, songs, and airs for solo instrument.

Thereafter he was constantly productive, even if—in later years—he took his careful time. Only a few of those who listened to his first opera, *Oberto* (premiering on November 17, 1839), would have survived to hear his last. *Falstaff* premiered in his eightieth year, on February 9, 1893, and—like *Otello*'s before it—the opening performance was a much anticipated cultural event. When he expired at eighty-seven, the composer and his second wife (the singer Giuseppina Strepponi, dead four years earlier) were celebrated as national treasures. Although he had requested a small and private funeral, there was a second internment—a thoroughly public occasion:[1]

> More than 300,000 people paid reverence to him on that day: the funeral car, towering more than 4 meters above the street, looked like a black and gold boat sailing on a sea of humanity. It was drawn by six horses, draped in black. Six carriages with wreaths and floral displays followed. Before the cortège left the cemetery, Toscanini conducted a chorus of 820 voices in "Va, pensiero" from *Nabucco*. After it reached the Casa di Riposo, the Miserere from *Il Trovatore* was sung. In the procession were a royal prince, the Count of Turin, representing the

King and Queen; consuls from several European governments; the presidents of the Italian Senate and Chamber of Deputies; many members of Parliament; the Mayor and city officials of Milan; delegates from every other major Italian city; several cabinet ministers; Puccini, Mascagni, Leoncavallo, Giordano, and scores of other professional colleagues; the Conservatory faculty and student body; a squadron of lancers; a band; a large corps of mounted police; the entire city fire department; and, immediately behind the funeral car, members of the Verdi, Carrara, Barezzi, and Strepponi families. *L'illustrazione italiana* noted that no priest accompanied the coffins. All along the route, tapestries, flags with mourning ribbons, and coloured silk hangings were displayed from windows and balconies. People everywhere were leaning from rooftops and clinging to the branches of trees.

Only a handful of artists so entirely embody achievement in old age. Verdi's final operas, *Falstaff* (completed when he was seventy-nine) and *Otello* (written six years before), are at least the equals of his youthful work, and arguably the capstones of his musical career. As experiments they register stylistic advance—intense and compressed by comparison with, say, the expansiveness of *Aida* or *Don Carlos*. Upholding the primacy of voice and the dominance of diatonic melody, they nonetheless juxtapose solos, duets, and ensembles in surprising ways. Few operas have such a feel of urgency as does *Falstaff* in its opening bars. (The initial gesture in *Otello* feels somewhat similar: a *tutti* eleventh chord hurled forward in syncopation as the action starts.) No such thing, here, as an overture or prelude or introductory choral arrangement; Verdi cuts straight to the chase. There are seven bars of *fortissimo* music, then rapid dialogue; he has dispensed with the paraphernalia of more traditional performance and embraced the unexpected—the embellished cadence and often unorthodox linkage of third-related chords.

Both *Falstaff* and *Otello* are forward-facing ventures, if distinct from the "progressive" music being promulgated in Germany and France. The tension generated between melodies and the chords that support them is characteristic of Verdi, as is his sense of how to color a given dramatic situation. The harmonies are richly chromatic, their tonal register suggestive, and there's no diminution of "the Maestro's" theatrical flair. Whether "chromatic or diatonic, decisive or evasive, conventional or unusual, the power of his music derives from his power of selection."[2] The score abounds in purposeful discontinuity, but always in the service of the dramatic situation: Sound and sense are one.

These operas use Shakespeare's plays as story line (*Falstaff* more freely than *Otello,* since its basis is the less-hallowed *Merry Wives of Windsor*), and Verdi contemplated yet another adaptation—of *Antony and Cleopatra*—with his last librettist, Boito. This additional venture did not come to pass. Indefatigably present at rehearsals, importantly involved in every aspect of production, the octogenarian might have concluded that another such endeavor would have been too much. (Much earlier, in his mid-forties, he had contemplated and then given up on *King Lear*. And he was less than satisfied with his revised *Macbeth* in 1865.) His final works—the *"Ave Maria," "Stabat Mater," "Laudi alla Vergine Maria,"* and *"Te Deum,"* collectively known as *Pezzi Sacri*—are scored for voice and orchestra. The *"Pietà Signor"* (1894), on which he did collaborate again with Boito, was a contribution to an album for the benefit of victims of an earthquake in Calabria and Sicily.

Indeed, and though "no priest accompanied the coffins," it's fair to say that Verdi's previous "Requiem" (1874) and the *Pezzi Sacri* (1889–1897) blur and then eradicate the line between sacred and secular devotion; his religion all along had been the making of music. When Desdemona sings her *"Ave Maria"* in Act IV of *Otello,* the high strings with which the recitation begins are juxtaposed, though five octaves below, to the upward-swelling double basses that announce her husband's entrance, blade in hand. Her recitation and prayer are the stuff of theater at least as much as worship, and the

"Bacio" figure from the love duet of Act I is repeated—beautifully, hauntingly—as her life draws to a close.

What strikes me as worth stressing, therefore, is not so much departure as the *sameness* of the enterprise, an unyielding and consistent faith in transcendent sound. Most careers have high and low points, a *succès d'estime* and then *succès fou* as well as a failure or two. And Verdi's is no exception; his sojourn in Paris was, by and large, a period of disappointment, and he wrote several works that were ill received. Few opera companies today perform such ventures as *Alzira, Aroldo,* or *La Battaglia di Legnano;* time winnows chaff from grain. *Un Giorno di Regno,* for example, was a fiasco in 1840, whereas *Rigoletto,* first performed in 1851, continues to delight. Of the quartet in the last act, the composer remarked to Felice Varesi, his Rigoletto, that he could never do better. Yet on and on he wrote.

To the very end, as one biographer puts it:[3]

> Verdi was, however, composing. It was the habit of a lifetime, and he would never altogether lose it. He once had written Mascheroni, the conductor: "Every man has his destiny: one to be a donkey all his life, another to be a cuckold, one to be rich and another poor. As for myself, with my tongue in my mouth like a mad dog, I'm fated to work to the last gasp!"

Further:[4]

The patriarchal boy is the final manifestation of a man whose character was indomitable, volatile, who could not be exhausted by the struggles for his art, whose intense activity extends almost uninterrupted through 70 years, having begun when he was thirteen (in that year, 1826, Beethoven bade farewell to art with his Quartet op. 135, and Weber lay dying, having staged his *Oberon),* and only effectively ending when he was 84 (when Puccini and Strauss were already famous, Debussy's star was rising and Schoenberg was composing *Verklärte Nacht*).

As a personality, "the Maestro" stays opaque. Most of the testimonials published in his lifetime hover near idolatry. Here, for example, Felix Philippi, a journalist for the *Berliner Tageblatt,* describes a meeting with the eighty-six-year-old Verdi in terms that can only be called hagiographic. Nonetheless it's worth quoting at brief length because it represents a widely shared reaction to the composer:[5]

> ... never in my life have I met a man of such serene, or rather, such transfigured appearance. Successes and triumphs, you will say, have ennobled his soul. I have known other geniuses, whom the wave of

fortune has raised as high but who have shown no "transfiguration" and not even gratitude. Verdi was a genius with the soul of a child. The chasteness of his thoughts, the purity of his feelings, his charm, his forbearance, his artistic and human morality were wonderfully moving. His whole being resembled one of those beautiful tunes he sang, one of his sweet and tender melodies devoid of discord, resembled a still, unruffled mountain lake, from whose clear depths golden treasures gleam.

Others called him secretive, severe. For such a public presence he stayed resolutely private; there are questions he never would answer and answers he never quite gave. The matter of Strepponi's illegitimate child, the truth of an affair with the singer Teresa Stolz, his response to negative reviews or journalistic diatribes—all these and more remained, in the composer's presence, off limits. No stranger could gain access to his private life or the procedures of his study. Those who expected wit and *joie de vivre* in Verdi report instead on his calm reticence, his laconic refusal at table to engage in gossip.

Some of this no doubt has to do with the distance he traveled from being a peasant child of illiterate parents to becoming a man whose birthday was acknowledged by a respectful king. (Indeed, the chorus of *Nabucco* became a kind of national anthem, so the Italians—singing Verdi—were spelling out *Vittorio Emannuelle Re di Italia*.) And a remnant of the small-town small-time wariness stayed with him to the end. When he purchased a gentleman's farm and used it as an annual retreat, he employed his father there, a reversal of authority that could not have come without cost. Of *Il Trovatore* he wrote to a friend, "People say the opera is too sad and there are too many deaths in it. But after all, death is all there is in life. What else is there?"[6]

Yet his final opera places the Lord of Misrule, a jocund fat man, at its center and in the title role. Shakespeare's Falstaff accurately asserts, "I am not only witty in myself, but the cause that wit is in other men." And he seems to have given Verdi a great deal of sport in the making; the fugue with which the opera ends has the refrain *"Tutto nel mondo e burla"*—All the world's a joke. What gladder way to quit the stage and, soon, the concert hall?

• • •

Francisco José de Goya y Lucientes was born on March 30, 1746, in the province of Saragossa, Spain; he died on April 16, 1828, in Bordeaux, France. Having outlived his social circle, he in any case withdrew from it; his burial was private and his passing unremarked. As the example of Beethoven posits, few physical afflictions do more to isolate the sufferer than does the loss of hearing, and Goya grew deeply distrustful of the world he'd reveled in when young. The sometime darling of the court and chosen portrait painter of society's great lords and ladies became "the deaf one," *El Sordo,* the haunted fabricator of *Los Caprichos, Desastres de la Guerra, Los Proverbios,* and, finally, the black paintings. What had been exuberance became misanthropy; what once was cause for celebration became the occasion for grief. There is nothing so nightmarish in the history of visual art until Picasso's *Guernica*—and Picasso's debt to Goya (as well as Velázquez) has been long established. These three grandees of Spanish art are root, trunk, branch, and leaf of the one tree. Or, to shift the metaphor, the deafness and the darkness were born of sound and light.

But there had been bright light. For much of his early career, the ambitious and provincial boy reveled in the spectacle of daily Spanish life. Though a relatively slow starter, Goya honed his gift of accurate rendition, ranging far and wide for subjects, painting peasant and king, courtesan and soldier, pilgrim and queen. The world of the bullfight and palace and blacksmith's forge and cathedral furnished him with topics equally, and his attention seemed omnivorous: no person too lowly or high. Perhaps his most famous pair of portraits—*The Clothed Maja* and *The Naked Maja*—attest to this duality; he could paint a woman resting, dressed, and (somehow less erotic) paint her nakedness as well. Goya's energy was boundless and his productivity huge; in this he resembles less his austere predecessor Velázquez than his successor Picasso. With oil paint and charcoal and etching tools he memorialized the life of Spain and also its obsessive dance with death.

Of the twenty children he made with his wife, Josefa Bayeu, only one outlived him; of the notables he painted only a few retained power; one of his great portraits—of the actress Dona Antonia Zárate—shows her dying of consumption and made pale by that wasting disease. With time the character studies give way to caricature; the face of the beautiful Duchess d'Alba becomes the two-faced slattern of *Los Caprichos*—and I mean the image literally: In *The Dream of Lies and Inconstancy* the woman looks both ways.

This was a turbulent period, with shifting political alliances and threats of persecution; Monday's favorite at court might well be, by Friday, in exile or dead. By the time of Napoleon's wars and the massacres in Madrid (on the second and the third of May 1808) Goya saw death everywhere and everywhere recorded it: on roadside and hillside, in bedroom and field. His vision had grown both clouded and clear: The haunted creatures and fantastical scenes all seem somehow familiar. If Hieronymous Bosch imagines hell, the Spaniard appears to record it, and his series of etchings and black bleak last oils make of the human comedy a farce.

How did this happen, we cannot help wonder; why did the well-paid purveyor of portraits to nobility become so fierce a critic of the idle life? How did the nubile maiden grow so coarse and leering; when did the agile youth become a stooped and toothless man? In part, no doubt, such disillusionment is a natural aspect of aging; the more he saw the less he liked, and "scales fell from his eyes." In part, as well, this could have been a function of incremental deafness—which some ascribe in Goya's case to a severe lead poisoning from the oils with which he worked. At the least his loss of hearing would have canceled early pleasure in conversation and music; the depression that assailed the painter in the early 1800s and again in 1819–1820 may have been causal too. In the terms of contemporary psychology we might call him a manic-depressive; the leveling rage and *bonhomie* seem two sides of the one coin.

Few figures so well documented are so contradictory, and it's hard to get a clear-cut picture of the man. Some contemporaries call him cautious, even miserly; others describe him as profligate and ready for a brawl. Some call him a man of the people; others point to his acquired "de" ("de Goya y Lucientes" as he styled himself in later age) as an attempt to gain nobility; his turn-by-turn allegiance to a separate set of monarchs is considered authentic or feigned. Of his willingness to work for the French-imposed ruler, Joseph Napoleon,

Juan José Junquera writes: "It is consequently difficult to know what Goya really thought, what his position was on what was happening, or what was his true political outlook, which he was so adept at concealing."[7]

A man of great physical force and resilience, he's known for his collapses and long convalescence; one of his most moving paintings (*Self-Portrait with Dr. Arrieta, 1820*) shows Goya at death's door. By all accounts a doting and generous father of his surviving son, Javier, he's unforgettably the painter of Saturn devouring a child. Most biographers claim the artist was an enthusiastic womanizer and in love with the Duchess d' Alba; others say there is no evidence of an affair. And if—as does seem likely—the two of them were lovers, who tired of whom is unclear. The widower's longtime housekeeper, Leocadia Zorrilla de Weiss, is alternately described as his attractive, kind mistress or a domineering shrew. Her daughter Rosario is sometimes thought to have been the artist's love child; others call this a romantic legend, and unsupported by fact. Even his supposed quarrel with the Duke of Wellington (Goya reaching for a pistol, his portrait's subject for a sword) may be attributed to deafness and mere misunderstanding. The iconography of the "black paintings"—indeed, the whole question of whether or not there *is* an iconography and set of embedded intentions—stays subject to debate. The images, as Sánchez Cantón describes them, are difficult to read.[8]

> Commonplace mythological subjects—Saturn, The Fates—and Judith the well-known biblical scene, alternate with realistic ones, sometimes brutal, and sheer fantasies. The attempt to organize them into a system of transcendental thought with a preconceived plan behind them seems to me completely opposed to Goya's temperament and art. He was an artistic, not a philosophical, genius, with more feeling and imagination than ideas, and those ideas he had were neither very clear nor very deep, let alone systematic.

These "black paintings"—so labeled only after his death—filled two floors of the *Quinta del Sordo,* the house that "deaf man" Goya purchased on the outskirts of Madrid. He bought the house in 1819 and departed for Bordeaux (his first trip outside of Spain) five years thereafter, in 1824. At the beginning of his residency, he was well past seventy, and during that first year fell ill. What these pictures represent is darkness visible.

There are fourteen separate compositions, painted directly on the walls and wall hangings, in the mode of his apprentice frescos, though by the time of their conception he was anything but an apprentice and had long mastered technique. Nonetheless, one senses a terrible impatience with everything that impedes or obstructs the making of his images; they are over-painted, often, and composed in seeming fury if not haste. The house itself has been destroyed and the paintings removed (with considerable damage) to the walls of the Prado, but it's almost unimaginable to imagine having lived with them: the ravenous ogre engorging a child, the mired men fighting with cudgels, the lonely yearning dog. *The Witchy Brew*—two elders huddled by a bowl—*The Ministration*—two women watching a man masturbate—*A Final Pilgrim*, and *The Fates and Their Creation* and the rest all hover at the edge of madness, an apocalyptic landscape inside of which it must have been near torture to exist.

This sensibility is, of course, a very modern one. Goya anticipates the look and feel of painters such as Francis Bacon, and one need only consider the aesthetic of his near-contemporaries to see how future-facing was *El Sordo;* nothing remotely like his etchings or late oils were current at the time. As Robert Motherwell observed, "An American artist of the twentieth century feels much more identification with Goya than with the Impressionists. Americans are not familiar with the world of pleasure, simplicity, sensuality that was part of the French bourgeoisie of the nineteenth century."[9]

As early as February 6, 1799, the *Caprichos* were announced and advertised in *Diario de Madrid*. They would go on sale two weeks later, their fanciful grotesqueries contained in eighty prints:[10]

> The artist, being persuaded that human error and vice may be legitimate subjects for graphic art, just as they are subjects of oratory and poetry, has selected from innumerable follies common to mankind, as well as from those lies authorized by custom and ignorance, those that he considers appropriate to ridicule.

By and large this "ridicule" was first confined to graphic art, the smaller and more private mode permitting an expressiveness that gave only abstract offense. He could not risk the disapproval of those patrons he was painting and on whose sponsorship he still relied; there's a kind of disconnect between the lavish oil portraits and the renditions of "error and vice." And yet he did put them on sale. Unlike the scrupulous precision of the *Tauromaquia*—a set of quasi-documentary reports on the technique of bullfighting—these etchings seem conceived in a rush and done with a broad stroke. For once the artist permitted himself to vivify his anger, its expression grew unstoppable, and it becomes the dominant mode of Goya's later life. To some degree his English equivalent would be William Hogarth, but Hogarth's excoriations of society in *A Rake's Progress* and elsewhere carry with them a grace-note of the reformer's conviction that things can be improved. Not so in Goya: Hopelessness and horror are what he sees and shows.

The final series of etchings—designated during his lifetime as *Disparates* and later as *Proverbios*—are even more a flagellation of humanity's stupidity. As one of his biographers writes:[11]

> The *Disparates* were the last and the most profound of Goya's messages to mankind. They were a rebel's last will and testament. In addition to the mischievous pleasure he had taken in concealing their true significance, he made their mystery denser still by contemporary and personal allusions, unintelligible today. This is a message written in code; and in spite of the effort of a century, the key has not yet been found. The *Disparates* have kept the savor of a secret half-divined.

Self-portraits too grow secretive and difficult to read. In the half-open eyes of the invalid artist (*Self-Portrait with Dr. Arrieta*) we imagine what the old man sees, staring forward with blurry precision. This painting repays close scrutiny; its inscription reads "Goya, with grateful thanks to his friend Arrieta for the skill and care with which he saved his life during the acute and dangerous illness suffered at the end of the year 1819 at the age of seventy-three, painted this in 1820." The doctor props his patient up on what is clearly a sick-bed, cajoling and half forcing him to drink what must be medicine. Their two heads are adjacent, the younger man's expression fierce as well as gentle. Household attendants watch. Goya rests in the doctor's embrace. Yet there's a seeming reluctance to come back to life, a yielding to such ministration only from exhaustion, a desire perhaps to be released from those internal and quasi-infernal tableaux; the doctor as savior condemns his patient to survival, and to the man being succored it's a mixed blessing at best.

In one of his final oil paintings, however, the pattern is reversed. What we saw in Giuseppe Verdi is a constancy if not repetitive consistency; this artist by contrast would alter his worldview with age. And at the very end he did so once again. Five years subsequent at least to the *Self-Portrait with Dr. Arrieta*, and perhaps Goya's last completed canvas, comes the astonishing *The Milkmaid of Bordeaux*. In March of 1825, Leandro Fernández de Moratín mentions in a letter to his friend Juan Antonio Melón that Goya has purchased a shawl. Quite plausibly it's the shawl being worn by his model (whose identity remains unknown, though romantic conjecture suggests that it's Leocadia's love child, Rosaria). The picture stands in such tonal opposition to the nightmarish black paintings that some believe it not by Goya, as if he could no longer capture the aspect of innocent youth. Yet each brushstroke argues mastery, a peace that passeth understanding and pleasure in roseate flesh.

The composition is simple, the background a wash of color, and the only detail rendered beyond her face and clothing is the milkmaid's urn. Her brown eye broods, her lips are pursed, her hands invisible. The woman takes her momentary ease, her head half bowed, reflective, perhaps a little melancholy; her full bosom and her ruddy cheek attest to wholesome health. It is a vision of beauty—*Et in Arcadia Ego*—that one hopes might have abided for the old man mad about painting; to have witnessed and produced this girl is a satisfaction, surely, and "doth redeem all sorrows that ever I have felt."

That phrase from King Lear's dream of a revived Cordelia proves delusional, however; the truth of the father's farewell scene is "Never, never, never, never, never." Goya's milkmaid of Bordeaux is the very stuff of reality-based fantasy, and all the more consolatory for what went before.

· · ·

Third member of the trio—both the youngest and most recent of the figures in this chapter—is Giuseppe Tomasi di Lampedusa. Unlike his two predecessors, however, and over the course of his lifetime, the last prince of Lampedusa remained, as an artist, unknown. Importantly too, as distinction, he came from the nobility and not from a farmer father, as did Verdi, or a working gilder, as did Goya. The vector of his public profile is downward-facing, not up; no solemn parade or mourning crowds commemorate his death. Born on the island of Sicily two days before Christmas in 1896, the prince breathed his last in Rome on July 23, 1957, at the age of sixty.

Reticent, even reluctant, he came to the work of prose late; alive, he published next to nothing: three articles of literary criticism in 1926 and 1927, on such subjects as the "archangel" Keats and the Italians Petrarch, D'Annunzio, and Leopardi. Then Lampedusa composed no more (with a view to publication) for nearly thirty years. In his mid-fifties he began to write in earnest, but his masterpiece, *The Leopard* [*Il Gattopardo*], appeared only after his death. Thus he furnishes a kind of bookend to the sad history of Hölderlin, whose best work appeared early on and who wrote mainly doggerel for the second half of his life. This writer's is a story of major achievement at career's close, even if the achievement itself went unrecognized.

A couple of caveats here. First, his relatively young demise makes him technically ineligible for my gallery of portraits. Lampedusa succumbed to cancer closer to the age of his beloved Shakespeare than that of the octogenarians Verdi and Goya. And Shakespeare, dead at fifty-two in the seventeenth century, would have been comparatively older than a man of sixty in the mid-1900s. So what we're dealing with is "lastingness" in the sense of a vocation found near life's end and not in the first flush of youth.

By all accounts, however, Lampedusa was an "elder" almost from the start: a shy man, and aloof. This had something to do with patrician reserve, a sense that very few—beyond the members of his family—deserved his confidant's attention or camaraderie. Formal, habitually silent, he made no small talk and seldom made friends. In photographs he's the plump young man in a military uniform, sporting a mustache; later, smiling, smoking, he's the stooped grandee. Eyewitness reports are, by and large, unimpressed: The prince is that portly gentleman nursing a cup of coffee at a corner table in a neighborhood café, the one at the edge of a party, the one with his nose in a book.[12]

Lampedusa's shyness did not diminish as he grew older. He felt at ease only at home, at Capo d'Orlando or with young people interested in history and literature. In other circumstances acquaintances remembered little about him except his large pallid

appearance and the fact that he seldom spoke. It was
the same whenever he met people in public, whether
at the Bellini club, a cocktail party, the Caflisch café
or the film society: an ironic smile, a few monosyl-
lables and nothing more. When he was introduced
to people, he shook hands without looking at them.

Married, he was childless and lived for long stretches
apart from his wife; their letters attest to cordiality but no
sort of physical passion. His passionate devotion attached
to his mother instead. Further, the prince adored pastry
and homes in the country and dogs. According to his
biographer, David Gilmour, he seems to have decided
to undertake fiction because his equally eccentric and
learned cousin, Lucio Piccolo, garnered some praise for
some poems—and it occurred to Lampedusa that he
could do as well and might just do the same.

So the whole notion of "career" must be in this case
redefined. His single book is, roughly speaking, all we
have, and cannot therefore be compared to what he
wrote before. Heir to a great name and a great squan-
dered fortune, the prince never worked for a living; his
one job (which he accomplished dutifully) was as an
organizer for the Red Cross in the province of Palermo,
after the Second World War. He studied literature in
several languages and wrote exhaustive notes—of
which more later—for a series of lectures delivered to a

coterie of young men. Yet he neither aspired to nor succeeded in the role of professional author, and if he felt deprived of recognition did not betray disappointment. In his final days, after a pair of rejections from publishers, he wrote to his adopted son: "I would be pleased if the novel were published, but not at my expense."[13] There's pride here, and integrity, but not a careerist's ambition. And Lampedusa would have been surprised by his posthumous success:[14]

> In November 1958 the first edition of *The Leopard* was published in Milan. It was an exceptional novel, wrote Bassani [Georgio Bassani, the book's editor] in the preface, one of those works which required a lifetime's preparation. A fortnight later an enthusiastic review in *La Stampa* set the book on its path of extraordinary popularity. In July of the next year *The Leopard* won the Strega prize, Italy's leading award for fiction; by the following March, it had gone through fifty-two editions.

Few novels of the twentieth century—Proust's, perhaps, and Robert Musil's—stand in such splendid isolation or are so completely achieved. Capacious in its reach, detailed in its descriptive precision, retrospective as well as predictive, in every way a work of full artistic maturity, *The Leopard* feels like the distillate of generations and, indeed, a nation. If Sicily were to be contained within and represented by the pages of a single text (as is the case for Colombia and Marquez's *One Hundred Years of Solitude),* it would be Lampedusa's. He did what he set out to do, and more.

The Risorgimento, the rise of Garibaldi, his invasion of the island in 1860, the declaration of Rome as the capital of Italy ten years later: All this furnishes the backdrop for a domestic "decline and fall." As an evocation of landscape—its sound, sight, feel, taste, odor—the book is without peer. Powered in part by nostalgia for the world of his dead ancestors, in part by disgust at the future they would usher in, Lampedusa's novel gives a panoramic overview of society: aristocrat and *parvenu* in their fateful yet fated embrace. The portrait of "the leopard" himself, Don Fabrizio (based on the writer's great-grandfather, the astronomer Giulio di Lampedusa), is one of the great rounded portraits we have; the figure of his nephew Tancredi is incandescent as well.

Another Italian aristocrat, Luchino Visconti, made an epic film of *The Leopard,* conveying both its sweep and scope and displaying with his expert's eye the look of that lost world. Claudia Cardinale and Alain Delon play the parts of the young lovers, but Burt Lancaster—an unlikely seeming casting choice for Don Fabrizio and, apparently, Visconti's choice only after Olivier turned him down—steals the show. His ramrod-straight posture and physical bulk somehow incarnate the unbending Prince of Salina, and to the degree that his character "bears an awful resemblance to myself"[15] (as Lampedusa wrote his friend Guido Lajolo), the mannerly disdain and prideful nostalgia ring true. So does the far-seeing gaze, the chill assessment of motive, and the pervasive despair. The author's long indictment of Sicily, its history and morals, reads like a family quarrel, timeless in its anguished wrangling with a time gone by. Perhaps the best-known line in the book is Tancredi's ironic pronouncement that "if we want things to stay as they are, things will have to change." And, somehow confirming that paradox, this record of a society's change preserves things "as they are."

What I want to focus on, however, is less the substance than the style of composition; this chapter celebrates the triumph of three very different artists at their very different lives' end. For Lampedusa fuses, in his debut effort, the affirmation of old Verdi and the negation of old Goya—all the more impressively because, as craftsman, he was starting out and not continuing what had gone before. Once *The Leopard* had been drafted, he taught himself revision, and though he had long meditated these pages they bear traces of apprenticeship. After completion of his novel, he wrote a few short stories (one of which, "The Professor and the Siren," is impressively accomplished) and began a second book.

Yet the output is small, the additional reach modest, and were it not for *Il Gattopardo* we'd not be reading him now.

A lifelong bibliophile, the prince was an omnivorous reader all along. But the making of fiction failed to engage him, except as scholar and teacher. He kept notes, for the purposes of discussion and dissemination, on writers such as Austen, Brontë, Dickens, and Scott; he praised the writings of Walton, Defoe, Swift, Richardson, Fielding, Sterne, and Johnson; the English novelists of the twentieth century he admired were Conrad, Joyce, Virginia Woolf, Evelyn Waugh, and Graham Greene. "I am a person," wrote Lampedusa in 1954, "who is very much alone. Of my sixteen hours of daily wakefulness, at least ten are spent in solitude. I do not claim to be reading for all that time though; sometimes I amuse myself by constructing literary theories. . . ."[16]

One could write a separate study of those "literary theories" and the lectures he prepared. "The two principal pupils for Lampedusa's course in English literature were Francesco Orlando and Gioacchino Lanza, though some of their friends were also present at the lessons on Joyce and T. S. Eliot."[17] Apparently, the prince composed his talks in the afternoons before lessons began; they took place three times a week and lasted into the night. He would discourse in chronological order on, among others, the Venerable Bede, Sir Walter Raleigh,

John Dryden, the metaphysical poets, the Romantics: Keats, Wordsworth, and Coleridge. He gave a whole series of lectures on Shakespeare, each of the plays and poems, a set of talks on relatively minor writers such as Ann Radcliffe, Matthew Lewis, and G. K. Chesterton; he did the same for French literature, admiring Montaigne and the authors of the Pléiade as well as Rabelais, Balzac, and Stendhal; he displayed, in short, a dazzling array of information and conveyed it with good humor to his attentive listeners. The notes amount to more than a thousand pages of learning worn lightly and comprise, in effect, a devotional commonplace book.

Here's a representative passage, in which Lampedusa declares his "subterranean love" for *Measure for Measure*:[18]

> If someone told me that all the works of Shakespeare must perish except one that I could save, I would first try to kill the monster who had made the suggestion. If I failed, I would then try to kill myself. And if I could not manage even this, well, then, eventually, I would choose *Measure for Measure*.
>
> Superb, indefinable poem and great, unclassifiable work of theatre, it is too tragic for comedy and too ironic for tragedy, a play in which the most beautiful lines of poetry alternate with the harshest and most "haunted" prose. Like the Pietá Rondanini

which it resembles, the work displays in its rugged awkwardness dazzling signs of the most transcendental genius. . . .

For more than twenty years, as well, the prince meditated on the prospect of a book about his ancestors. He did write a memoir of childhood, evoking the houses his family lost: the country home at Santa Margherita (sold to strangers, and enlarged into Donnafugata for *The Leopard)* and the palace in Palermo, bombed during the Second World War. There's charm here, and pictorial precision—Lampedusa was an enthusiastic if dilettantish photographer—and a gallery of servants and relatives and furniture and suppers and journeys by carriage described. The pages are carefully composed and the recall near total, but nothing in it quite prepares us for the absolute assurance of *Il Gattopardo* itself.

In January 1955 he learned he had emphysema, and though this did not immediately read as a death sentence it did make him husband his energies and commence to work.[19]

He started writing with diffidence. "*Je fais ça pour m'amuser,*" he told Licy [his wife], and when Pietro della Torretta asked him what he was doing, scribbling away, he replied, "Enjoying myself." Yet this nonchalance was a pretense. Once he had taken the decision to start, he committed himself to his writing. During the last thirty months of his life, he worked almost every day on his novel and stories, writing painstakingly in a blue biro at a table at the Mazzara café or in his library at home.

It's worth repeating that what he wrote was the distillate of a lifetime's worth of experience as well as reading; he did prepare himself in Yeats's "singing school." Still, there's something remarkable about the image of an elderly gentleman in a café, drinking his coffee and water and nibbling at pastry and producing, page by page—in a mode he'd never attempted before—a major work of art. If "lastingness" can be in part defined as that which survives its maker, *The Leopard* is a paradigmatic instance; Lampedusa near life's end both imagined and recorded a lost, enduring world.

In mid-June 1955, while working on the memoir *Places of My Infancy,* he makes a declaration. After praising the prose of Stendhal: "…what lucidity of style! What a mass of reflections, the more precious for being common to all men!" he writes:[20]

I should like to try and do the same. Indeed it seems obligatory. When one reaches the decline of life it is imperative to try and gather together as many as possible of the sensations which have passed through our particular organism. Few can succeed in thus creating a masterpiece (Rousseau, Stendhal, Proust) but all should find it possible to preserve in some such way things which without this slight effort would be lost for ever. To keep a diary, or write down one's own memories at a certain age, should be a duty "State-imposed"; material thus accumulated would have inestimable value after three or four generations; many of the psychological and historical problems that assail humanity would be resolved. There are no memories, even those written by insignificant people, which do not include social and graphic details of first-rate importance.

One can only speculate on what it cost the artist to have his work rejected—twice!—by publishers just before he died. He must have known that his "material thus accumulated would have inestimable value"; he must have known that what he knew was of an order of magnitude greater than those who failed to recognize the "first-rate importance" of his prose.

CHAPTER SEVEN

The Idea of Continuity

Sweet hours have perished here;
    This is a mighty room;
Within its precincts hopes have played,—
    Now shadows in the tomb.

                    Emily Dickinson

Max Eastman was in his eighties when I was in my twenties; we met on Martha's Vineyard and grew close. He welcomed me, whether in Gay Head, Manhattan, or Barbados; he was tolerance incarnate, with an amused abiding sense of how youth preens. In addition to his work as activist and editor, he had published more than twenty books—volumes of poetry, biography, and political commentary, as well as a set of translations from the Russian; the second installment of his autobiography, *Love and Revolution: My Journey through an Epoch* (1964), seemed a title entirely earned.

I postured. I was working on a novel *(Grasse 3/23/66)* that was recondite in the extreme. I'd labor in an ecstasy of self-congratulation, producing perhaps a hundred words a day, intoning the sibilant syllables until they appeared to make sense. One such passage, I remember, contained a quotation from Villon; a description of Hopi burial rites; an anagram of the name of my fifth-grade teacher; an irrefutable refutation of Kant; glancing reference to Paracelsus; suggestive ditto to my agent's raven-haired assistant; paraphrase of the dirge in *Cymbeline*; and an analysis of the orthographic and conceptual distinction between Pope and Poe.

I took my time; I let it extend to ten lines. That night I brought my morning's triumph to Max and permitted him to read. He did so in silence. Then he tried it aloud; so did I. When he said it made no sense and I explained the sense it made, he looked at me with fond exasperation. "Sure," he said. "That's interesting. Why don't you write it down?"

I remember staying with him on Martha's Vineyard one October. His wife, Yvette, was off to New York for a shopping trip, and she asked me to sleep in their house—a favor to me, really, since my own hut was unheated. I was full of beans and bravado then, and would get to work by six, waking up and clacking at the keys in my upstairs bedroom. In the first pause, however, I could hear his steady hunt-and-peck in the study underneath; he'd been at work well before. So we'd share a cup of coffee and a comment on the news, then I'd fuss at my novel again. At nine o'clock I'd take a break, tear off my clothes, and run down the hill to the pond. The morning would be glorious: that crystalline light, those sizeable skies, the pine trees somehow greener against the sere scrub oak. And always, out there in the still warm water, Max would lift his hand to me, his white mane on the wavelets like some snowy egret's, grinning.

Time passed. He died at eighty-six, in 1969. But it takes no effort to see this again: an old man waving from the water at a youth on the near shore. They are naked, both of them; the sun slants over Lobsterville. A few day sailors might be on the pond, or someone in a kayak, or musseling, or digging clams. Gulls drift past, incurious; the beach smells of sea-wrack and weed. There's a busy imitation of silence: the man in the water, bobbing, flutters heels and hands. The young one runs to meet him and it's all a perfect clarity until he does a surface dive and, splashing, shuts his eyes.

• • •

What do I see when I shut them; why is it simpler to focus with closed eyes?

His was a vivid presence and mine is a good memory; did I get it right?

For time is the great editor; it makes us revise and revise.

"But it takes no effort to see this again: an old man waving from the water at a youth on the near shore...."

I first composed this testimonial for a book of photographs in 1977, called *On the Vineyard*; I also used it in the introduction to a text I edited, *Speaking of Writing,* in 1988. The former contained a set of essays by some-time residents of Martha's Vineyard, the latter a series of Hopwood Award Ceremony lectures, one of which was delivered by Max as long ago as 1932. I further adapted the five paragraphs with which this chapter starts for an essay called "Letter to a Young Fiction Writer" that appeared in a collection of the same name in 1999.

I repeat myself now in part because the passage seems appropriate and I like the lines. More importantly, I continue to honor my old mentor's memory and hope to keep his name current. Also germane to this fourth usage in this fourth decade is the fact of recurrence, the almost obsessive variation on a verbal theme. There are a few small revisions of what I wrote before, some cutting and trimming for context, but in essence it's the same five hundred words.

What does such repetition suggest; why should the image recur?

And now that I am closer to Max Eastman's age than that of his companion, how might I (re)write the scene?

What of the smells, the sounds?

The temperature?

Was it fresh water or salt?

When Claude Monet painted his three-hundredth canvas of a water lily, was he merely repeating himself? When Shakespeare repeated the phrase "time's fool," was he being formulaic? I do not of course compare my work to that of those great artists, but the problem is analogous; once you establish a mode of expression, what yield is there in change?

Max Eastman's body no longer exists; my own has trebled in age. In my mind's eye, however, he is alive and I'm young.

•   •   •

Brain and *body* have long been perceived as opposing entities, but also as closely allied. *Mens sana in corpore sano*—the Roman pairing of "Sound mind in sound body"—is an ideal still widely endorsed. In different contexts, this duality has different names (spirit and substance, intelligence and instinct, sacred and profane, otherworldly and secular, soul and flesh), but the dichotomy persists. Often as not the conjunction employed is *or*, not *and*—as in "intelligence or instinct," "sacred or profane." And much of our hunger for lastingness seems a search for reconciliation, a desire for the two to fuse. Is it "mind over matter" or vice versa or "mind and matter" conjoined?

This study deals with Western models of achievement, Western artists in old age. It's my anecdotal sense, however, that other cultures deal with the disjunction more easily and with a good deal less fuss. The physical and spiritual impulses feel somehow attuned in a yoga adept or tribal chieftain or medicine man. When Prince Gautama renounces wealth or an Inuit elder walks out on the ice, there's a traditional-seeming willingness to say "Enough's enough." No doubt this very statement is romantic, uninformed—but the stages of enlightenment in Buddhist and Hindu nations are more closely calibrated to increasing age than our "retirement policies" in the capitalistic West. We're better at getting and spending, in short, than at renunciation, and little in our history urges the reverse.

Are we "hardwired" for this somehow; what evidence accrues? What, if any, biological explanation is there for the loss of artistic achievement in increasing age? We understand that our generative fertility decreases—in both women and men—as we grow older; does this mean our creative fertility also must diminish? Is there a region of the brain for art (some sort of left-or-right-lobe equivalent for control of the imaginative faculties) and does it lose force? If so, is that loss foreordained or can it be forestalled? Weighing in at roughly two percent, the brain uses twenty percent of our body's energy; is this a constant ratio or could it be changed? Might we dissect the "gray matter" of Pisanello or Purcell and discover where genius comes from, and of what it consists?

Here it helps to have some understanding—however rudimentary—of the structure of the brain. The cerebellum, the brain stem, the frontal lobe, the parietal lobe, the temporal lobe, the occipital lobe, the primary motor cortex, the primary sensory cortex are its principal component parts; they have separate regulatory functions and "responsibilities." The parietal lobe, for example, is where letters form words, and words combine into thoughts; the temporal lobe regulates language and learning, the occipital lobe processes information related to vision. All these are necessary for the production of art; they are not sufficient.

Here, in layman's language, is a functional description of the full-grown (roughly three-pound) brain itself: "The brain receives information from our senses (eyes, ears, skin, balance organ, muscles and joints, nose, tongue), uses it to detect, represent as neurological activities, recognize, and record memories of the things of the world, and employs this information within, and outside of the domain of immediate time, to develop and guide our mental and physical actions. Incoming information is pre-processed in the great sensory systems that feed the 'forebrain.' That 'forebrain' fills nearly 90% of the volume of our skulls. No mammal has a larger one than we humans in proportion to our body size. The forebrain is comprised of a great assembly of special 'sub-cortical' brain regions that feed and support the analysis and action functions of about a hundred distinctive functional zones in our highly-folded 'cerebral cortex.' The cerebral cortex is a thin (about 1/8" thick), layered structure about two and a half square feet in area (imagine a circle a little less than 2 feet in diameter). Within this thin sheet, there are about the same number of neurons (nerve cells) as there are stars in the Milky Way—about 20 billion, of the brain's total of about 100 billion."[1]

Following is a brief time line of discoveries in Europe and Egypt relating to the mind:

In a skull dating from 5000 B.C., there is evidence of trephination: a hole cut through the skull. This practice—persisting through the Middle Ages—is used to treat headaches or seizures.[2]

Ancient Egyptians discard the brain when mummifying corpses; the brain—or so they believe in 2500 B.C.—is unimportant by comparison with those organs preserved in their canoptic jars.

Hippocrates (460–370 B.C.) describes epilepsy as a physical disorder, not something occasioned by the displeasure of the gods. He believes the brain to be the seat of emotion and intelligence.

Herophilus of Alexandria and Erasistratus, his student, are the first to rely on dissection, in 300 B.C. They describe the nervous system.

The physician Galen dissects the brains of animals—sheep, monkeys, dogs, and pigs—and distinguishes, in 170 B.C., between the cerebellum and cerebrum.

Thomas Willis, an Oxford professor, writes *Cerebri Anatome* in 1664, the most detailed description until that time of the nervous system. He believes separate parts of the brain are responsible for thought and movement.

In 1668 Johann Jakob Wepfer proposes that stroke may be caused by a broken blood vessel in the brain.

In 1791 an Italian physiologist studying frogs—Luigi Galvani—is the first to suggest that some form of "animal electricity" drives nerve activity. Hence our word "galvanic."

In 1808 a German anatomist, Franz Joseph Gall, creates the pseudoscience of phrenology—insisting that a person's personality can be revealed by the contours of the head.

In 1870 Camillo Golgi develops a staining method that reveals the detailed structure of sensory nerve cells in the brain.

Emil Kraepelin, in 1883, describes schizophrenia and manic depression.

William James publishes *Principles of Psychology* in 1890; Sigmund Freud nine years later publishes—as part of his ongoing inquiry—*The Interpretation of Dreams.* Ivan Pavlov explores conditioned responses in 1903; B. F. Skinner in 1938 argues that animal behavior can be engineered.

In 1906 Alois Alzheimer details presenile degeneration—giving his name to the disease as of 1910.

From lithium to lobotomy, there are available treatments today for bipolar disorder and psychosis. We have begun to track the neural pathways of the brain, as well as its plasticity and ability to regenerate. Prozac and other drugs have been approved as a treatment for depression; electroshock therapy and brain scanning and gene therapy have been introduced. Great breakthroughs are occurring in our study of the organ; the understanding of its function is in flux. Some forty years ago, a scientist might well have been expected to know *all* the literature on the structure and operational functions of the cerebellum and cerebrum; now these articles multiply exponentially and no "unifying theory" has as yet emerged.

Further, it seems fair to say that nobody has yet proposed an explanation for what we loosely call "inspiration" or—at its outer edge—"genius"; we cannot locate, in the brain, that place where creativity exists.

This last statement is not strictly true; we do in fact know roughly where images—and, by extension, the imaginative faculties—reside. What we don't understand as of this present writing is why one individual can make of his or her imaginings an enduring work of art and another puts away her pencil or his brush. A separate study might be made of those whose parents and grandparents had been writers, painters, and musicians; is there a genetic component involved, or is it instead an issue of environment and encouragement? When Lucas Cranach the Elder taught Lucas Cranach the Younger to draw, or Wolfgang Amadeus Mozart played the piano for his father, was this a function of nature or nurture, and in which proportion? The sons of football players and the daughters of ballerinas may have, as it were, a leg up on the competition, but this doesn't necessarily mean they will surpass their parents or colleagues in the same field. The determining word here is *talent,* and it can be identified and supervised but not engineered.

• • •

What I've been trying to describe is our incremental awareness of the function of the brain itself, as well as its relation to the body that encloses it. Our most important organ, it's the one we understand the least. An aging artist—male or female—must contend with failing physical resources, but the failure of human alertness is difficult to measure and very hard to chart. We're familiar with memory loss and the distinction between short- and long-term memory, that "senior moment" when we forget dates or names. Our ability to learn languages and calculus, not to mention downhill skiing, diminishes with time. But what happens when our cognitive abilities themselves commence to fade; are they in some way replaced? And since the creative impulse is so readily accessible in the young, why has it been censored in the old?

Infants and children acquire skills rapidly; the brain's capacity quite literally enlarges—as do our hands and feet. Proportionally less expansive than other parts of the body, it nonetheless does grow. So at what point, as a general rule, does the counter-contraction begin? At forty, sixty, eighty; *is* there a general rule? There are those who argue that our life span can be indefinitely extended, and that entropy—the process of structural collapse—can be reversed. But we need not live forever to live longer, and there's no obvious reason why the "sunset years" must mean a reduction of light.

If our natural life span expands and life expectancy increases, might not consciousness do so as well? Can we replace discovery with knowledge, exploration with perspective? We have more information to absorb and process than did our ancestors; does that mean we are better equipped to manage the workaday world? Most contemporary citizens of the United States know how to operate a telephone and computer and drive an automobile; does that make us more intelligent than those who arrived on the *Mayflower* or braved the western plains? Or have we lost as much by way of programmed reflex (the ability to sail by dead reckoning, the ability to track wild animals, the aural retention of long sacred texts) as we appear to have gained?

Let me stress what should be clear; these questions are a good deal harder to answer than to ask. It's possible that some years hence some genome project of the brain will decode its signals as successfully as has been done for our genetic markers and DNA. And no doubt then we'll know much more about the wellsprings of artistic growth, their source as well as stanching. But at this stage it would appear that knowledge of the brain does not advance an inquiry into "lastingness" as such. Neural transmitters and the release of chemicals such as dopamine and noradrenaline and acetylcholine are crucial to a study of brain function but inadequate as explanation for why and how well we make art.

Rather, the creative process involves a separate and equally inexact attribute of behavior: "character."

That configuration of response to stimuli we define as "character" or "personality" has more to do with artistic production than the cerebral cortex in its operational modes; the word retains its mystery and is hard to plumb. One of the phrases attached to the idea of character, for example, is that it takes time "to build." So too does a career, and the vicissitudes of time and chance have much to do with both. Such terms as *talent, personality,* and *character* are nonscientific, but no analysis of brain waves or ocular perception has managed to explain the work of Dryden or Poussin.

Another way of putting this is, in effect, anecdotal. The writer in his sixties says, "I could never have written this novel twenty years ago"; the painter at seventy-five declares, "I wouldn't have produced this painting when I was in my thirties"; the composer in her eighties hears a different tonal register than does the forty-year-old. It seems self-evident that life experience should be an important component of art; even in that most abstract mode of expression, music, we "read" romantic grief or revolutionary fervor or a birthday gift of melody to a beloved consort. And it's therefore natural that the work of older artists has a different feel and flavor than that of their earlier work. The "summing up" or "final achievement" of any creative intelligence is necessarily a function of increasing age, and only when a life is truncate does it apply to the young.

Is there a kind of poem, painting, or sonata that typifies the youthful maker or signals, instead, middle age? Is there a form of expression that requires, as prerequisite, the long view of the elderly? Outsider art and folk art and the artistic expressions of the insane are more difficult to date than those of the formally trained and technically proficient women and men who produce signature work. Can we carbon-date the maker as well as the thing made?

• • •

James Hillman, in *The Force of Character,* has a useful way of discussing the issue:[3]

> In our competitive societies, "lasting" has come to mean outlasting. "I've outlived my father and both grandfathers!" "According to my doctor, I should have been dead three years ago." "My insurance company is losing money on me. I've beat my pension plan and cashed in on Social Security, far more than I ever put in." Surely goodness and mercy shall follow me all the days of my life, because my life has outlasted the expectancy curve....
>
> Our experience of aging is so embedded in numbers of years left to live, as given by longevity tables, that we can hardly believe that for centuries late years were associated not with dying but with vitality and

character. The old were not mainly thought of as limping toward death's door, but were regarded as stable depositories of customs and legends, guardians of local values, experts in skills and crafts, and valued voices in communal council. What mattered was force of character proven by length of years.... Cemeteries were dotted with the short graves of children.

Further:[4]

Old English manuscripts love *eald* (old); it is one of the fifty most frequently appearing words in the medieval corpus of legal, medical, religious, and literary texts and occasional scribbles. And it mainly carries a positive meaning. Of forty-nine compound words that incorporate *eald,* only eight are clearly negative, like "old-devil." To include *eald* in a compound generally brings benefits: trustworthiness, venerability, proverbiality, value.

What Hillman praises, in his book, is the contribution made by those who represent tradition and who pass it on. Societal elders *should* be highly valued, and he therefore considers the retirement community (where the aged and infirm meet only those of their own generation) to be a bad idea. The "force of character" seems crucial here; one definition of the word is "a printed or written letter, symbol, or distinctive mark."[5] And that "distinctive mark"—the Greek root of the word *karakter* means "inscribed sign"—may prove very hard to erase.

Marcel Duchamp, for example, chose to abandon his public position as artist and turn his attention to chess; his character by all accounts stayed the same. The painterly achievement was established early, but inventiveness continued—even flourished once he put away those "childish things," the constructions intended for show. Born in 1887, Duchamp died in 1968, and for the last fifty years of his life played chess with the focused attention he had earlier accorded Dadaism. Such pictorial innovations as *Nude Descending a Staircase* and *The Bride Stripped Bare by Her Bachelors, Even* gave way to a study of gambits and traps, but the spirit of playful disruptive inventiveness stayed with him till the end.

This seems particularly the case for those whose art is self-reflexive and who make their own work consciously a topic. Thus when René Magritte inscribes *Ceci n'est pas un pipe* adjacent to the image of a puffed-on pipe, he's eating his cake and having it too. "This is not a pipe," admittedly, but it does picture that object exactly; it's both denial and affirmation in the comic mode. Laurence Sterne's whimsical extravaganza, *Tristram Shandy,* is composed in a similar vein; the portrait of the Widow Wadman (a blank sheet of paper, where the reader might imagine the lineaments of beauty) or of a character's grief (a black sheet) is an eighteenth-century display of narrative intrusiveness—the self-effacing storyteller who takes center stage.

There are many such examples. The music of John Cage offers an aural equivalent, yoking improvisation to measured repetition. The prose of Samuel Beckett (*Endgame* is a tip of the cap to the contest that compelled Duchamp) insists on iteration, and often humorously. "Let us leave these morbid matters, and get on with the fact of my dying," as one of his characters says. The entire system of *trompe l'oeil* is organized around the notion that you see what you're not seeing, and this taking-back what's been taken away is a hallmark of the elegy—a way to retrieve what was lost.

Johannes Brahms had the habit of revision—a quasi-compulsive revisiting of finished work, a dissatisfaction with all previous performance. His use of transposition (from chamber ensemble to full-fledged orchestra, from violin to clarinet) argues a similar cast of mind, and his Variations on a Theme by Haydn makes something original of something borrowed. A number of authors write sequels, returning to their characters some twenty or thirty years later or dealing with new generations of an imagined clan. Self-reflexiveness seems habitual for both the young and old creative intelligence, though it's not perhaps as common in the middle aged. Many

artists learn their trade by copying the work of predecessors they admire; Pablo Picasso referenced Velázquez
often, as did Édouard Manet. This is less surprising in
the apprentice than the master craftsman, but it holds
true for both. Near the end of his career, Picasso produced both a set of variations on the work of other painters (Goya, Rembrandt, Velázquez) and a set of graphic
studies of the naked artist with a model in his studio,
the priapic body thumbing its "nose" at convention.

Any discussion of "lastingness" cannot ignore this creative personality; he occupies stage center in the history
of twentieth-century art. Perhaps no other painter has
been so uninterruptedly fertile, or worked so hard so
long. The Protean shape-shifting inventiveness and prodigious output, the prolixity of styles and modes are all
beyond compare. But for that very reason I have left him
at the canvas edge; he seems exempt from useful scrutiny and renders comparison moot. What can one learn
from Picasso except that it helps to be born with preternaturally keen eyesight, the gift of agile draughtmanship,
and constantly renewed supplies of energetic ambition?
What moral can one draw except that competitive wrangling and brilliant innovation and sexual careerism may
coexist? To admire the thing made—consider the art
of Richard Wagner or Louis-Ferdinand Céline—is not
necessarily to admire the maker; creative excellence and
excellent behavior need not be joined at the hip.

Still, on and on he labored. On and on Picasso drew.
Just before his ninetieth birthday, for example, he produced six large paintings in less than a week—three of
them known as the *Three Ages of Man* and measuring
almost six and a half feet by four and a half feet. These
he completed by laying them flat on a table and standing
poised above them like the very lord of creation. *Rise,
genius* is an anagram of *sui generis,* inalienably a thing
apart, and this painter was one of a kind. The eyes of
his last subjects—whether toreadors or musketeers or
women—are nearly all Picasso's own eyes, according to
his biographer John Richardson, and make it look "as
though he is outstaring death."[6]

A common denominator of the final years would
seem to be just such a constancy of purpose, a tem-
peramental (often ill-tempered) stick-to-itiveness that
denies decline. The admiring comments "But he seems
so *young*" or "She's so *energetic*" contain at least an over-
tone of the condescending reverse: "Why don't they
act their age?" There's a complicated back-and-forth
of patience and impatience, the forward-facing and the
conservative impulse; we desire both repetition and to
start out anew. At a certain stage in Dante's progress,
Virgil bade the voyager farewell, and part of the lore
of "old masters" is that revelatory moment when the
teacher instructs his or her disciple to go ahead alone.

And if that *fails* to happen—if the teacher stays in lockstep with her students, insisting on being a part of the party—things feel in some way wrong. Had Virgil accompanied Dante all the way through "Paradiso," his traveling companion might well have complained. The stereotypical image of the aging artist as *monstre sâcré,* a satyr-like devourer of admiring youth and beauty, seems somehow apposite here. Drama and folk tales abound in such figures—the old man and young girl or boy, old woman and lithe acolyte—who suck life blood from their follower-victims and are, like Dracula, renewed.

Yet if "time is the great teacher," a senior artist *ought* to have earned wisdom to impart. She or he may grow more venturesome, less trammeled by propriety—even literally incontinent—once there seems less to lose. It's not only the young artist who seems iconoclastic or speaks truth to power; those who approach the end of life often do the same. Here too there's a kind of defiance, a variation on the theme of "Death, where is thy sting?" Leonardo da Vinci died at sixty-seven, but his self-portrait in "old age" looks utterly unsparingly at wrinkles and white hair. What I've been trying to suggest is how these strategies wrest gain from loss, spin gold from straw, make something enduring of what feels fleet. And this is the reward accorded those who spend their life in art: For a brief period, and possibly far longer, they are *not* the fools of time.

. . .

A great composer whose music languishes unheard, a writer or painter whose work is unknown belong to separate categories, as do those who labor for their own private pleasure or stay resolutely amateur. Some sort of public engagement seems a necessary precondition of after-the-fact analysis; the creative men and women I portray in *Lastingness* are those who once enjoyed, no matter how transient or fleeting, a modicum of fame. There are exceptions, of course; Hölderlin had no such awareness and Lampedusa knew no success. But artists rarely think of critical reaction or audience responsiveness as crucial to the work.

And even when they do so, it's a personal wrangle and private affair. Political and social agendas bulk less large. "Be careful what you wish for," as the adage has it; there's a turning away from the kind of approval once sought. Almost one senses an impatience with renown, a feeling—as with O'Keeffe, and Goya—that the prominence hard labored for bore real attendant cost. Writers such as Émile Zola or Upton Sinclair, painters such as Jean-Louis Forain or Honoré Daumier did use their skills in the service of reform, yet their need to write or draw was not, I'd guess, qualitatively other than that which engendered the work of nonprogrammatic or "abstract" artists. The act of bearing witness, once stripped to its essentials—a line drawing or a line of prose—pertains to each and all.

Giuseppe Verdi stayed secretive and Franz Liszt walled off by acolytes; the bluff Catalan Pablo Casals wintered in Puerto Rico with his much younger wife. Henry James complained of poverty but managed to employ a cook, a gardener, and a secretary; very little of his day took place—except when he desired it—away from the desk. Indeed, one of the things to note about the majority of our figures is how carefully cared for they were in old age—whether by family members, romantic partners, or a retinue of servants; they don't seem to have spent much time on doing the dishes or mowing the lawn. A generous way to interpret all this is that the senior artist focuses his or her attention on the quintessential act of making something beautiful; less generously one could claim that all the cosseting and cordoning off is a kind of tribute paid by protective attendants to the golden goose. But however one describes it, and whenever possible, the old practitioner expends less energy on the business of daily life; others shoulder the burdens of "getting and spending" while the worker works.

• • •

The elderly, or so it seems, repeat themselves. Children and grandchildren say or think, exasperated, "Come on,

I've heard that before." In the case of senile dementia, such repetition can grow obsessive—a few catchphrases caught in the throat, a needle that slips in its groove. But almost everyone becomes to some degree formulaic, saying the same thing in separate ways and even, at times, word for word. Is this a necessary component of "lastingness"; does repetition inescapably attach to continuity—as with the work of Beckett or Mark Rothko or John Cage? When a painter paints the sunset or a soup can more than once, when a composer elects the same key, is that a failure of inventiveness or witted variation on a theme?

One of the advantages of a number of books on the shelf is that the writer comes to recognize a pattern in his or her writing; old subjects do recur. Lately I've taken to slipping youthful passages verbatim—a sentence, often, a paragraph sometimes, at the outer limit a page—into the present work. I own those previous books, after all, and (as with the memory of Max Eastman with which this chapter starts) there's a kind of time-lapse photography involved. I won't sue myself for copyright infringement, and if we all repeat ourselves, not meaning to, why not do it consciously instead?

It's a private salute to the idea of continuity, a sense that repetition's unavoidable in any case; why not acknowledge it, therefore, and, if you liked the phrasing once, use it again. *It's a private salute to the idea of continuity, a sense that repetition's unavoidable in any case; why not acknowledge it, therefore, and, if you liked the phrasing once, use it again.* Or perhaps it's more accurately a sort of self-transfusion, a desire to be jolted by what felt electric years ago. In a recent work of fiction, *Spring and Fall*, I included a sequence from a novel of mine that came out in the early 1970s and a line from a short story that appeared in the mid-eighties. They slipped, I think, seamlessly in; they snuggle between the covers where nobody else recognized they had lain before.

Now let me explicitly repeat the final lines of *The Lost Suitcase*, a novella I published in the year 2000. It's about an old, much-honored writer who loses sight of—falls afoul of—his muse. He's living in retirement in somewhere I imagine to be something like Key West. His name is Edward, his inspiration AnnaLise, and here's that novella's last page:[7]

> ...And therefore bit by bit and almost imperceptibly over time our hero—once so severe, so constant of purpose and disciplined in habit—permits himself to take her not so much for granted as for something of less value than it was to start with: a currency debased. Soon what has begun as attitude becomes a routine condescension, a familiarity that serves him as first cousin to contempt. A diminution of his capacity for wonder, a sense there's nothing singular

in being singled out like this and that she is but foot-
note to his text.

Till one fine morning he wakes up and, as always,
stretches and, as always, shifts the pillow and thrusts
back the blanket and gets out of bed, gingerly test-
ing his right leg, his hip, the stiffness in his joints, the
muscles of his back, his throat engorged, his mouth
still tasting like the bottom of a birdcage, and shuf-
fles to the bathroom where he runs the tap and spits
and rinses off his teeth, blinking, pissing, hawking
phlegm, and turns on the overhead light and switches
on his own electric kettle for the first cup of hot water
with lemon, since he does not want to bother the night
nurse or, more precisely, to be bothered by her, cannot
bear to a share the fuss and ruckus of conversation at
this hour but instead surveys the landscape (sea grape,
sea fog, the rising sun and fading moon and could that
be the Southern Cross?) and throws back the green
wooden shutter and latches it, as always, to the black
hook in the stucco wall and sits to his work desk, as
always, positioning the cane-backed chair, sharpening
his pencils and smoothing out the foolscap and reading
what he wrote before, the verbiage accumulated yesterday and also the day before that, sucking maybe on
a gumball, staring at the palm tree and the cactus there
beyond the pool, sitting poised as though expectant of,
attendant on *her* visit, her seductive tactile presence on

the naked yellow unlined sheet. For he has worked this way for months, for years, for decades, every morning in this fashion at this hour and no matter what has gone before, how hard the night or troubled the sleep, how many words he wasted on and with how many incidental players, undone, unstrung, half-comatose, so that it is merely accurate and neither boastful nor self-serving to report the yield was real, the harvest abundant, the language *available* to Edward—witness the books on the bureau, the awards and plaques on walls, the shelves in the library bulging—and therefore it takes him longer than it should have, possibly, to sense how something else obtains this day, some alien vacancy enters the room, or how the light comes slanting in without illumination.

The palm trees do not frame his view, and what he has for company is absence and not presence.

Not AnnaLise.

The habit broken, the pattern no longer ingrained.

The song he taught himself to hear is silence now, not with him now, not this fine morning at his desk and—although he does not wish to admit or consciously consider this he knows it already, irrevocably—once gone it is gone and will not return to him ever, nor come to him again.

As once in May.

CHAPTER EIGHT

Gratification

...Courage is no good:
It means not scaring others. Being brave
Lets no one off the grave;
Death is no different whined at than withstood.

Philip Larkin, "Aubade"

When I began this book several years ago, I thought the figure just described was representative—that "Edward" and his brethren were not the exception but rule. By now I'm not so sure. In fact, I have come to believe the reverse: The older artist need not be a monstrous amalgam of ego and need, a drunk or incompetent fool. As most of my portraits suggest, it's possible—perhaps increasingly so—to change in fruitful ways with age, to equate maturation and growth. Therefore the list of "Enemies of Promise" with which this text commenced now seems to me more properly a problem attaching to youth; that's what Cyril Connolly focused on in 1939.

What his excellent study discussed, moreover, were the pitfalls and pratfalls of early success; my own concern is with endurance and, from time to time, advance. Although *Lastingness* now nears its end, it's clear the inquiry into late style and its expressive opportunities is only just beginning. Actuarial tables and medical treatment and the unprecedented comforts of contemporary existence all suggest we will continue as a species to continue; life spans have been increased (in the world's affluent societies) and death postponed. Jaques's "many parts" from *As You Like It* need no longer be confined to "seven ages"; they can well expand to nine or ten, and each act may extend. Before the turn of the twentieth century, the issue didn't loom as large; now there are exponentially more elders than was the case before. So it's, in effect, a new subject; what earlier had been remarkable has become routine. And when those who live past seventy persist in their creative work, "the art of old age" is an ongoing challenge, not something past and done.

What lessons may be learned?

First, the process is rewarding no matter the result. "Process" stays more or less constant, though the terms of engagement may change. In this book's opening chapter I briefly described the behavior of my father, ninety-eight, and father-in-law, ninety-four. The former lived a private life, the latter still a public one, but in both instances it's clear that the pleasures provided by painting and music outweighed the sorrow of lessened effect. I mean by this that Greenhouse knows his hand is no longer strong enough and his agility too limited for solo concert performance. Yet music-making in and of itself sustains him; indeed (as with Casals) it keeps him young. My father in his final months spent hours of rapt study regarding an etching or drawing by some much-admired predecessor, then making his own marks upon the sketchbook sheet.

In this regard, perhaps, the artist has a better chance of engaged old age than the retired business executive; once an "occupation's gone"—Othello's great lament—our satisfaction in the workaday world is also effectively over. Not so for the elderly painter who could complete his canvas no matter what the weather because he worked at home; the nonagenarian performer can still sit to his violoncello although no longer onstage. When I contemplate retirement (after more than forty years of teaching) I think of it as the opportunity not to improve my golf game but to spend more hours at the writing desk; the page beckons just as seductively and dauntingly as was the case decades ago.

•   •   •

Second, and related to the first, is the whole question of "result." Is the measure of success an objective or subjective one, and what objective measurements should be brought to bear? Titian's late paintings are splendid, but are they better than his early or mid-career accomplishments, and in whose opinion? Might that verdict be appealed and the judgment change? When, six years before he died, Titian reworked his great *Christ Crowned with Thorns,* did the new canvas register growth? And does such alteration in itself matter more than continuity; is it always positive? Change can mean loss as often as gain; as the psychologist Erik Erikson (1902–1994) and others remind us, things alter willy-nilly. None but the early dead escape the stages of age.

We've grown accustomed, as a culture, to the rapid turnaround and constant replacement of starlets and stars; best-seller lists prove unreliable as an index of what lasts. The graph of a career is rarely a straight line; more often it's a bell curve of ascendancy, then slow subtraction: a valley and peak. What goes up will come down. There's seldom a one-to-one correspondence between intrinsic value and the degree of success; most men and women who persist in their endeavors will follow a pattern of commercial rise and fall. But the twenty-year-old and the eighty-year-old are necessarily dissimilar in their relation to these matters, and a first encounter with public reaction is different than a fifth.

The hunger for applause may never be sated by feeding, and even a much-honored person may take umbrage at a slight. Certain men and women require the spotlight to shine. But more and more, it seems to me—at least on the basis of those creative personalities here profiled—gratification turns inward. Incrementally, the making of the thing itself displaces its reception; reviews and sales and standing ovations come to matter less. I refer here yet again to the distinction between public and private; in the former context repetition can grow burdensome, in the latter it's a gift.

This holds just as true, of course, for those who are not artists. The simple fact of waking up and watching light suffuse the sky, of drinking a first cup of coffee or tea and dressing or walking without pain—the comfort conferred by long habit is available to all. A pattern of extended life does emphasize process over result, the pleasures of "more of the same."

Further, each creative act stands distinct from its available effect; it sometimes seems as though the act of *making* and the act of *showing* belong to two different categories and systems of behavior. The publicity tour and gallery display are almost entirely separable from that which first engendered them. (An exception is performance art. What used to be called a "happening" is by its nature over once the occasion has happened, and every performance—improvised as well as rehearsed—is to some degree affected by audience response. An actress knows her work is finished when the curtain falls; a playwright may hope for productions to come.) And the elderly maker, it would appear, has a better-proportioned sense of what is or isn't possible in the work's "afterlife." Perspective does improve.

In any case, things change. The whole idea of lastingness is value charged, a function of the fourth dimension, time. If what others think about one's work grows less and less important to the aging maker, he or she may labor privately and avoid display. It's easier, of course, to say this of creative personalities who *have* a reputation, but I would guess the same holds true for those without a major public profile in their final years. Stories abound of men and women who keep their late work close to home and even in some cases hidden; J. D. Salinger, we're told, composed many thousands of pages he didn't deign to publish, and Goya's black bleak paintings were made for his own eyes alone.

The wall of silence protecting Salinger was rarely breached the last half of his life; as of his death at ninety-one on January 27, 2010, we do not know if what he wrote was gold or dross. Or even *if* he continued to write—though that had been part of the mythos from the time he withdrew to New Hampshire. By rumor he kept at his work desk, with no desire for public acclaim, producing quantities of language undisturbed. Quite plausibly the unpublished texts—presuming we do get to see them—will fail to withstand close critical examination; the warning signals (as of the long short story "Hapworth" in 1965) argue a kind of collapse. But that need not be true. It's at least a possibility that his late prose outstrips the early, and *Catcher in the Rye* or *Franny and Zooey* will come to seem mere warm-up exercises for the final triumphs secreted in the drawer.

As Anthony Storr observes, in *Solitude: A Return to the Self:*[1]

One of the most interesting features of any creative person's work is how it changes over time. No highly creative person is ever satisfied with what he has done. Often indeed, after completing a project, he experiences a period of depression from which he is only relieved by embarking on the next piece of work. It seems to me that the capacity to create provides an irreplaceable opportunity for *personal development in isolation*. Most of us develop and mature primarily through interaction with others. Our passage through life is defined by our roles relative to others; as child, adolescent, spouse, parent, and grandparent. The artist or philosopher is able to mature primarily on his own. His passage through life is defined by the changing nature and increasing maturity of his work, rather than by his relations with others.

Dr. Sherwin B. Nuland, in *The Art of Aging,* has this to say:[2]

Every culture associates being wise with older people, though it is well known that merely being old does not in itself confer wisdom, nor does being young prevent it.... Like aging itself, the having of wisdom is a stage of ongoing development, whose degree of success depends upon every other stage that came before it.... Whatever its degree of justification, the belief that wisdom is the province of age is reflected in many cultures, but in no language more directly than in Hebrew, where the word for "old," *zaken,* is an acronym formed from the expression, *zeh kanah hokhmah,* literally, "this one has acquired wisdom."

And Ronald Manheimer, as well, in *A Map to the End of Time,* charts the intersection of wisdom and old age:[3]

The philosophical tradition has long extolled intellectual contemplation (what the ancient Greek philosophers called *nous*) as the loftiest human attainment. Not mysticism's union with God, but *Sophia*, contemplation of universal truths, is the philosopher's goal. Another strand of the great tradition that sometimes complements, sometimes competes with wisdom about the grand order of things is what Aristotle, in his *Ethics*, called *phronesis*, "wisdom in action." This applied or "practical" wisdom involves our ability to exercise good judgment in matters of commerce, profession, friendship, family, and civic life. Underscoring the difference between the two types of wisdom, Aristotle observes that while "young people can become mathematicians and geometers and attain theoretical wisdom in such matters," they still do not possess practical wisdom, because it is knowledge gleaned through concrete experience that requires "a quantity of time." We should listen to older people, says Aristotle, "for, since experience has given them an eye, they see correctly."

•   •   •

Small dogs live longer than large ones; the life expectancy of a Chihuahua is, roughly, twice that of a Great Dane. Dwarf mice have greater longevity than their more sizeable counterparts, or rats. Yet they belong to one species, as do those men and women who live past the age of ninety or die by forty-five. Since the category *Homo sapiens* remains the same, it's a disparity within similarity, a distinction without difference. We're not, I mean, genetically programmed as human beings to give out at a certain date or continue until a date fixed.

Wilfred Owen died when twenty-five in one of the last battles of the First World War; Robert Graves survived his wounds and lived a long creative life, dying in Majorca at the age of ninety. Had the trajectory of enemy bullets been infinitesimally altered, the fate of these two poets might have been reversed. As the passage in Ecclesiastes reminds us, "I returned and saw under the sun, that the race is not to the swift, nor the battle to the strong...nor yet favour to men of skill; but time and chance happeneth to them all." Cholera, malnutrition, earthquakes, bombs—those accidents of "time and chance"—have more to do than we care to acknowledge with artistic production and lasting achievement. But if, benign, such accidents permit a man or woman to continue to work, he will acquire of necessity a sense of proportion not earlier present; she takes, as it were, the long view. And it's time now to consider what may, from that vantage, be seen.

• • •

Throughout this book I've danced a dance between the artist and the art produced, the maker and thing made. If process is what matters to the aging creative personality, then why not simply say it's fine to dabble at the limerick or whistle off key or mound round shapes in clay? Inward satisfaction can be real and rewarding even when the thing produced is minor or a mess. In the outward-facing sense of "lastingness," however, it's necessary to assess the effect of the work on others—its resonance and qualitative size.

And this is where aesthetic judgment enters in. A study of the forty extant Rembrandt self-portraits can't claim—on the basis of brushstroke or composition—that the final work improves on the early, or that the old man staring at himself is "greater" as painterly achievement than those oils that capture the young self-regarding gaze. It's not, primarily, a function of technique. What moves us so in the late-stage self-portraits is the unimpeded scrutiny of a visage "warts and all." Restiveness and vanity have been replaced; the artist in his studio at sixty studies himself in a different way. Less effort is expended on display and more on revelation. Less showiness, more shown. The light has changed, the costume darkened, flesh gone slack, and year by decade the self-portrait's proud precision fades till the face in the mirroring canvas looks inescapably other than the face in its fierce prime.

Bonnard, Picasso, Renoir, Rodin—every visual artist to whom I've alluded—changed their application of paint or wielded the chisel differently in their declining years. In truth, it would surprise us if that were not the case. To say that late and early styles are different things is not to say much new. In part this is a function of physical necessity, the loss of eyesight or motor control or simple impatience with detail (as in Degas's pastels or Michelangelo's slaves.) But another part of what we respond to is the view *because* occluded in the elderly practitioner; "whole sight" can grow dim yet stay keen.

Gabriel Fauré did change his style; Francis Poulenc did not. George Rochberg in his final period renounced the twelve-tone compositions that had been his chosen mode. Richard Strauss's last song-cycle is a triumph of a different order than was his first; his *Metamorphosen* exemplifies its title and embodies change. What, if anything, does this imply and why should we concern ourselves with the qualitative distinction? Perhaps it can suffice to say that value judgments of the hierarchical sort—this is *better,* that is *best*—are beside the present point, and what counts in late-stage artistry is, once again, the distance between intention and execution.

Did the painter or composer do what she set out to do; does the writer write what he wants?

The stages of an artist's life may well appear as definite as the years marked by a calendar, but at every age a marker of success for the productive personality is just such a personal estimate: *How close did I come?* Concomitant discovery—the accidents of sound and shape—can prove crucial to the whole; not every creative enterprise has been thoroughly preplanned. More often the reverse. But *Lastingness* has focused on the space between what was imagined and what was produced—the fusion, as it were, of process *and* result.

Many contemporary sculptors hire fabricators to realize maquettes; the aging Henry James dictated his books to a "typewriter," as he called his secretary. We have more and better enabling assistance for the work of hands. Yet even if construction of the artifact be delegated to others, the conceptual achievement belongs to its originator—as was the case with master and apprentice in a studio centuries ago. Although in small or sizeable ways the technologies may alter, it's still a function of pen on paper, brush on canvas, bow on string. Her signature, his fingerprint remains. This holds as true for an art form as for its individual practitioners; innovation is routine but the paradigm shift is rare.

A twenty-year-old graphic artist constructing shapes

on a computer has more in common with Piranesi and Bernini than might appear at first glance; the tools may differ but the impulse is equivalent, and when Richard Serra builds his complicated arrangements of steel he's engaged in a procedure not all that different in kind from men who worked with hammered gold in the sixteenth century. It stretches the point over-thin to say there's *no* distinction between those who labored on church doors and those who fashion plates of Cor-Ten, yet the difference has more to do with the resulting object than with the impulse to make it. So when critics label a piece of art Hellenistic or Baroque or Mannerist they're describing not the procedure but the finished thing; "result" is finally what matters to those who look, listen, or read—and a separate set of criteria must be brought to bear.

The apprentice and the journeyman and master craftsman are, I think, alike in this, and it's a useful way to measure artistic achievement. It obviates the questions of *size, rank, ambition*, and permits us to focus on yield. Too, it's a different kind of yardstick, or different form of measurement, than the one that charts public acclaim. "The dead don't care," writes poet-undertaker Thomas Lynch, but those who survive them care greatly, and memory persists. We read suicide notes with attention, unfinished drafts or snippets of verse for their predictive qualities and after-the-fact revelation; did X understand that these would be her final words, was Y conscious of a legacy, did Z hear the knock on the door?

Here it's important to distinguish retrospect from prospect; what we look back on now is what they looked forward to then. And this holds just as true for a bagatelle or symphony, a miniature or fresco, an epigram or epic. It serves no useful purpose to contrast an apple with a lamb chop, a *Moby Dick* with "Crossing Brooklyn Ferry." The former both are edible, the second both describe journeys by water; thereafter comparison ends. What's constant for the artist is this matter of intention, and it doesn't matter all that much if he or she elects to shift previous style.

As Rudolf Arnheim puts it, "The acuity of vision and the range of hearing decline, short-term memory begins to fail, reaction time lengthens, and the flexibility of intelligence gives way to a channeled concentration on particular established interest, knowledge, and connections."[4] Methodology also can change. The maker may offer up sketch after sketch, a lightning-quick composition or compulsive iteration of an unfinished phrase. It may be something wholly new or wholly recognizable, a variation on a theme or map of new terrain. But there's no prior standard—or none with which I'm familiar—that says *You must do this, you can't do that,* and to the degree that such standards pertain they partake of a formal rigidity. Melville broke rules; so too

did Whitman; a rule is there for breaking if the iconoclast is great enough, and no system of aesthetics can be
iron clad.

For one could claim that Schubert, before he died
at thirty-one, approached the matter of mortality with
just the soaring *gravitas* of Verdi in his eighties. The two
Piano Trios, the three Piano Sonatas, the Quintet in
C, and song cycles such as *Winterreise* are fully mature
compositions though produced when the artist was
young. Chopin too, dead at thirty-nine, built an extensive oeuvre, as if he knew his febrile lungs would offer
him scant leisure or the occasion to revise. The youthful
Keats was just as clear-eyed on the themes of life and
death as the octogenarian Hardy, and it may be that the
age of an artist while working is finally less important
than the number of years left for work.

In this mode of reckoning, the issue is not chronological age but, instead, how near to death. If one definition of a masterpiece be that it exists "outside of time,"
then the very question of who made it when becomes
less urgent. I have focused here, of course, on just such
a set of questions, but it should be admitted that excellence is rarely a function of clocks.

•   •   •

The obituary announcement of August 22, 2007,
brought news of the death of Grace Paley. She had been

suffering from cancer and was eighty-four. This was the second friend I planned to interview who died before I had the chance to schedule our discussion. The other was the painter Jules Olitski, also dead at eighty-four. Both, for me, were indomitable and long-admired elder presences; it's hard to accept them as gone. Their infectious energy and exuberant inclusiveness—as well as the work—will remain.

The last time I saw Jules he talked for literal hours, unstoppably engaged in memory and prospect. He was embarking on a new sequence of land-and-sky-scapes, and I believe his final paintings are among his best. The last time I saw Grace it was to drop her at an airport and watch her bantam figure stride purposefully off. This second loss brought with it the sad factual reminder that all plans are provisional and each career must end. Though I had conceived of *Lastingness* and commenced my research earlier, it was roughly at that moment I began to write this book.

When John Updike died at age seventy-six, on January 27, 2009, it was with work still to be published and some sixty volumes in print. He was my teacher at Harvard in the summer of 1962—the only time, to my knowledge, he taught. (He did once substitute for the indisposed John Cheever, but ours was a course he had signed on to offer; thereafter he removed himself from academe.) Updike lived on in Massachusetts as a private though increasingly public citizen, and we stayed in touch. I continued to admire him, to solicit his opinions, and therefore asked him the following questions on the topic of this text:

1. How have your work habits changed at present from the days when you were an apprentice to the trade?
2. How have your aspirations changed; do you think of a day's work as "more of the same" or have you set yourself different goals?
3. Can you point me to a passage—or passages—in your own writing which deals with these issues, either head-on or obliquely?

From a letter dated August 26, 2007, these are John's replies:[5]

1. When I was still a college student and then an employee for *The New Yorker* for twenty months, I of course fit my poetry and fiction into what gaps the traffic allowed, evenings or weekends. But once I left New York, in 1957, and set up shop as a free-lance writer in Massachusetts, with no other job, I tried to work faithfully, from breakfast to a late lunch, producing at least three pages a day, with whatever afternoon labors needed to be added. Fifty years later I am on the same schedule. In fact I seem to work

longer hours, perhaps because I am slower and/or more careful now, or more is asked of me—certainly book reviews did not take much of my time or energy until the 1960's. I don't have much advice to offer to younger writers, but when asked I do suggest setting a regular schedule and a modest daily quota, even if the day is low on inspiration. Make it a habit. The pages do accumulate.

2. The aspirations have not been dulled, but after years in the mines I am aware that my major veins have probably been dug out, and the urgency of my youthful "news" presses less groaningly. In the beginning, you are full, as they say, of yourself, and when elderly somewhat less so, having dispensed yourself through so many books. Still, each day slightly changes your angle on life, and the blank page remains a site of hopeful possibility. Some sentences as they take form still give me a frisson of pleasure. When the words quicken into what seems to be life, the writer is doing useful work. The little inspirations that used to feed poems and short stories don't come as often as they used to; I tend now to think in terms of books, each one possibly my last. The image at the end of all those hours with pen and pencil/typewriter/word processor is that of a finished book, with its beautiful trimmed edges and scent of fresh paper and binding glue.

3. The long essay on "Late Works"...dealt with the issues of longevity if not with lastingness. The way the individual investment in entertainment shapes up these days, the author does best who travels light— *The Great Gatsby* over Dos Passos's *USA*. But then you don't want to cater to a high-school reading level, and a certain capaciousness, involving the passage of time in its fabric, seems intrinsic to the novel. By and large what lasts best is the most concrete, the most actual, delivering to the reader a piece of earth and humanity. Aesthetic flourishes fade and wrinkle, though they may get attention when new. A blunt sincerity outlasts finely honed irony, I would think. An ability to see over the heads of important contemporary issues into the simple truth of daily life is what we can respond to a century later....

My own continuing to write at the age of three score and fifteen is a matter of genetics, long habit, and concrete aspirations. I set out to make a living with my pen, in privacy, in the commercial literary world as it existed, and am grateful that I managed. It's been a privilege and a pleasure, and it goes without saying that I've been lucky. No impairing disease. No war I was asked to help fight. No stupefying poverty yet no family wealth or business to limit my freedom. No appetite for fine living and racing sloops to assuage. Lovely bright loving parents, then good loyal women and healthy children living with me. *The New Yorker* when it still published many pages of fiction and Alfred A. Knopf Inc. when publishing was still a gambit for sensible gentlemen who trusted their own taste. A world where books were a common currency of an enlightened citizenry. Who wouldn't, thus conditioned, want to keep writing forever, and try to make books that deserve to last?

•   •   •

Many other authors were less willing to respond. I don't mean by this that they were churlish or ungenerous—only that they chose not to think of their career in these particular terms. William Kennedy at eighty, for instance, said he couldn't say anything useful; Joyce Carol Oates at seventy said, Let's defer the discussion awhile. And such a willed deferral is natural enough; most of us don't like to think we're engaged in or embarked upon our final act. When some medical condition declares itself, making finality the subject—a mortal illness, say, or a major pending operation—things shift. A death sentence of the actual or metaphoric sort does focus the attention, yet we tend to put off till the very last minute those reckonings we understand to be our end-point reckonings; *mañana* rules the day.

The letter from John Updike—and less formal exchanges with others—therefore comprised the whole of my "research" with elder artists still alive; it began to seem that in the very act of naming I subtracted their names from the list. The quick became the dead. When I asked about Grace Paley's health, planning to drive to her home in Vermont, my interlocutor said, "You'd better hurry." I didn't, and missed her—as also, a year earlier, I'd failed to interview Jules.

Nor were Paley, Olitski, and Updike alone. In the month I write this, the composers George Perle and Lukas Foss (both men I'd hoped to talk with) died. By the time this book sees print, the roll call will increase. As Dante puts it, in the *Inferno* (iii. 55–57) "*. . . si lunga tratta / di gente, ch'io non avrei mai creduto / che morte tanta n'avesse disfatta.*" In "The Wasteland," six centuries later, T. S. Eliot translated the line as ". . . so many, I had not thought death had undone so many." Or, to use James Baldwin's phrase, "the royal fellowship of death" has been much enlarged.

Within the last two years we lost Hortense Calisher, George Garrett, Elizabeth Hardwick, Anthony Hecht, James D. Houston, Norman Mailer, Arthur Miller, George Plimpton, William Styron, Arturo Vivante, and Kurt Vonnegut—all major figures in the world of words. The list reveals its maker; I knew them each, a little, and several of them well. Extend the "deadline" back a bit, and we could add Saul Bellow, Mona Van Duyn, Josephine Jacobsen, Donald Justice, Stanley Kunitz, William

Maxwell, Wallace Stegner, and Eudora Welty. (It's worth repeating here that I refer only to American authors who died in their seventies or older; the death of David Foster Wallace, for example, belongs to another discussion. So does the loss of Nobel laureates who lived and died abroad: Samuel Beckett, Elias Canetti, Naguib Mahfouz, Harold Pinter, José Saramago, Aleksandr Solzhenitsyn, and the rest.) Once they were marching in the vanguard; now they belong instead to those we leave behind. It makes a grim processional; the generation that succeeds them is the next to die.

•   •   •

Here, from a letter Vincent van Gogh wrote to his brother Theo, in 1886:[6]

> There is an art of the future, and it is going to be so lovely and so young that even if we give up our youth for it we must gain by it in serenity. Perhaps it is very silly to write all this, but I feel it so; it seems to me that, like me, you have been suffering to see your youth pass like a drift of smoke, but if it springs up again and comes to life in what you do, nothing has been lost, and the power to work is another youth.

The great painter shot himself at thirty-seven, ill and alone and ignored. It's the age of Aleksandr Pushkin, killed in a duel, the final age of Robert Burns. Toulouse-Lautrec died at thirty-seven, as did the incomparable Raphael, and—as I suggested at *Lastingness*'s start—we cannot know the ways the history of art would change had they grown old. When I think of my own history—a married father of two daughters at the age of thirty-seven, and living in North Bennington, Vermont—it seems both far away and long ago and almost entirely present. Time does contrive, as all of us know, to move both rapidly and slowly, and Faust's last pleading utterance, *"Verweile doch, du bist so schön,"* extended the vanishing moment—*Please continue, this is beautiful*—at the cost of his own death.

This was his "Faustian" compact, a promise to be kept. Once the moment feels so sweet its witness wants it to remain (according to Mephistopheles, who proposed the bargain), all our ceaseless striving will come to its earned end. It's no accident this happens to the old not youthful mage. A desire to capture what disappears, to fix in melody or line or language what otherwise is mutable—the creative urge to make a mark and have it persist—is deeply embedded in each of us; a chosen few may have that wish fulfilled. Faust himself was saved by the "good work" of his final achievement, and the productive end of his life redeemed what went before. Archetypical representative of Western man—with his perpetual dissatisfaction and constantly rekindled ambition—in the guise of the old artificer he figures forth the whole.

Johann Sebastian Bach (1685–1750) came from a family of musicians, and in his turn engendered them. His second son, Carl Philipp Emanuel Bach (1714–1788), for a period eclipsed his father in terms of reputation; the reverse is now the case. The older man, "to whom," in Robert Schumann's words, "music owes almost as great a debt as a religion owes to its founder,"[7] worked in relative anonymity if not obscurity; his fame has since enlarged. What many who love music hail as the noblest of all choral works, "The St. Matthew's Passion," was never once performed during the composer's lifetime. It took fully a hundred years after he had written it till an admiring Felix Mendelssohn produced this act of worship in Berlin on March 12, 1829, and there's no small irony in the fact of Mendelssohn's sponsorship; he was, after all, born a Jew.

Like several other preeminent artists (Da Vinci, Rembrandt, and Shakespeare among them), Johann Sebastian Bach did not survive to seventy. Yet when he died at sixty-five in the mid-eighteenth century, he would have been an old—as well as blind and apoplectic—man. To the very end, moreover, he persisted in his habit of enlarging and refining and codifying our creative musical tradition. Among his final efforts, *The Art of Fugue* (first printed in 1751, a year after the composer's death) exemplifies this process of inventive exploration. Its severity of logic and conceptual agility would seem astonishing in a precocious genius; in one so near the close of life, it beggars understanding. Bach was by temperament a didact as well as a rigorous systematizer; his *Pages from the Notebooks of Anna Magdalena Bach* or *The Well-Tempered Clavier* partake of this mode of instruction. He wanted to get it down *right*.

In *The Art of Fugue*, each of the fourteen examples (except for the final unfinished one) uses the same subject in D minor. As Christoph Wolff puts it, "The governing idea of the work is an exploration in depth of the contrapuntal possibilities inherent in a single musical subject."[8] There are simple fugues, counter-fugues, double and triple fugues, minor fugues (in which the score is inverted), canons, and an unfinished quadruple fugue—which breaks off in the middle of the third section, at the 239th measure. A mystery attaches to his use of his own name, B A C H, in the countersubject (H reads as B natural in English notation), since some suggest he died once having penned that phrase and in the very act of composition. Others argue—less breathlessly, more plausibly—that the finished fragment has been lost; still others theorize he left it purposively unfinished, so that those who follow after might continue with the technical investigation. Some call it a Pythagorean enigma; others a permutation matrix or an obsessive doodling. But whatever the truth of "*Contrapunctus XIV*," it's clear that Johann Sebastian Bach maintained his creative expertise and mastery of counterpoint. The mathematical precision and puzzle-solving aspect of his work does not diminish over time; what he built he built to last. As the organ or the violin or flute or violoncello or *Hammerklavier*—the soloist or aria group or hundred-throated chorus—perform his music now all over the world, we hear what the old master heard in the silent auditorium and echoing arch of his skull.

•   •   •

I commenced this set of portraits with the work of William Shakespeare, because it describes "the art of old age" for those who follow after. When Prospero declares, "I'll drown my book," he nonetheless does leave behind the ringing phrase that says so, and nearly four hundred years later we profit from the language with which Caliban was taught. Though the final line of *The Tempest* begs its audience to "set me free," the old artificer plans, as it were, to return for tomorrow's performance. The "farewell concert tour" or "Collected Works" is often as not a misnomer; the artist begins yet again. *Cogito ergo sum,* asserted Descartes, but *Continuo ergo sum* may also serve as motto: "I continue, therefore I am."

Let me repeat the definition in the O.E.D. of *lastingness* as "continuance; duration; permanence. Also: durability, constancy, perseverance." What my figures have in common is unabated desire, unflagging expressive ambition; old age slowed and changed but did not staunch their need to look, listen, or write. What they have in common also is unabated energy—at least in terms of the imagination and insofar as physically plausible. They kept on keeping on. Our artists, male and female, do share this attribute of *karacter* as *energeia,* both potential and kinetic: an unyielding fealty to the yield of work.

(A parenthesis here. Friederich Hölderlin's productive period ended soon, yet he persisted with his doggerel; no doubt it gave him comfort though the lines as such don't last. Goya's minuscule final enamels and Liszt's final piano pieces—no matter how contrarian or against the previous grain—still embrace expressiveness; they don't deny the importance of art. The only way to do so would be to renounce and even perhaps to destroy one's own work; that's a line in the sand these artists don't cross, and nothing in their long careers suggests a loss of faith in what it signifies to write, compose, or draw. The spirit continues willing, although the flesh grows weak.)

Early on I thought there might well be a single system within which to measure achievement—some single way to define the quality of lastingness and to describe its essence. The shape of a career, however, is always case specific. The individual excellence of these individual artists consists in large part of originality; while they may be representative they did their work alone. The various genres and various styles preclude any easy conclusion: It's not *one size fits all* or one way that's sure to succeed. The elder creative personality, therefore, won't march in lockstep any more than does the young painter, composer, or author. Had I reported on another ten or hundred figures I would have had another ten or hundred tales to tell.

Here's one. Gioacchino Rossini (1792–1868) made a career as composer, and was financially successful from the start. Among his operas are *The Barber of Seville, La Cenerentola*, and—in 1829—*William Tell*. Thereafter he retired, declaring he had earned enough and devoting himself to pleasure—principally, the delights of the table: eating, drinking, gourmandise. The recipe for Tournedos Rossini attests to his skills as a chef. In his long retirement he did produce some "sins of old age"— *Péchés de Vieillesse*—mostly for solo piano, but these were intended for private performance, and he seems to have departed the concert house and opera hall without regret. Wittily, Rossini said of himself that he wept only twice in his life—once at the end of the Mozart Requiem Mass in D Minor, and once when a truffled duck was washed overboard during a yachting party.

His is the exception, not rule. The sketches in this gallery report on those whose work advanced, or who made concerted efforts to advance their art. Late style can be reductive, in the sense of a refiner's fire melting off what's dross. It can be stentorian or assertive, in the sense of men or women with little patience left. It can take the long view or the near, the global or the local; it can expand or contract. But whichever the mode and whatever the mood it seems to me to demonstrate unrelenting passion, a conviction on the maker's part that art is what we have. Nothing digressive or languorous here, nothing that yearns for ratification or hungers for applause. Rather, the old painter, musician, and writer have a shared distaste for every interruption; rapt, they hunt the distillate of what they can that morning—or afternoon, or evening, or in the watches of the night—compose. The art of old age is discourteous; it has less time to lose.

CONCLUSION

Francis Steegmuller, a few hours before dying in a Naples hospital, said (presumably in Italian) to a male nurse who was cranking up his bed, "You have beautiful hands." A last, admirable catching at a moment of pleasure in observing the world, even as you are leaving it. A. E. Housman's last words were to the doctor giving him a final—and perhaps knowingly sufficient—morphine injection: "Beautifully done." Nor need solemnity rule. Renard recorded in his *Journal* the death of Toulouse-Lautrec. The painter's father, a known eccentric, came to visit his son and instead of concerning himself with the patient immediately started trying to catch the flies circulating in the sick room. The painter, from his bed, remarked, "You stupid old bugger!," then fell back and died.

Julian Barnes, *Nothing to Be Frightened Of*

This chapter's title is oxymoronic; it will not deal with closure. The subject of my inquiry is "that which does not end." But now that I'm several years into the project, I want to finish by beginning with a series of conjectures as to the art of old age—lastingness—itself.

To satisfy the reader and the writer, each text must reach a resting place; the end of any composition matters as much as the start. This holds just as true for music and the visual arts, where the finale is tonal or spatial; the resolution of a chord or color field provides the at-least-momentary comfort of a goal attained. "In my end is my beginning"—whatever its validity as a statement of belief—as an aesthetic assertion persuades. But in personal terms—and here again I intend the first person—the completion of a project is always grief-shadowed, a little; the distance between intention and execution looms large. I *could* have done this, I *should* have done that, I *failed* to include X and Y. Had I had world enough and time, I *would* have discussed A and B. So it's not perhaps surprising that a study of this subject should close by being open ended, or that its questions remain.

If art is long and life is brief, then what we make outlasts us. In flea markets and tag sales and antique shops there's a kind of afterlife on offer—some new potential owner assessing what was by others abandoned. The plates and cups and chairs and pots and carpets and

books and embroidered pillows and tables that some-
body's grandparents left behind are "collectibles" today.
Far from a culture of planned obsolescence we are, it
seems, a people bent on preservation; we don't throw
things away. And when we do in fact clean out the attic
or basement those objects get recycled; the plates and
cups and pillows arrayed on junk-shop shelves may well
be purchased generations later by those whose ancestors
first bought or sold or made them.

Such objects have lives of their own. Few violins are
played by just a single performer; few paintings hang in
perpetuity on a single wall. And the older and grander
the object the more completely this holds true; the pedi-
gree of a Guarneri "del Gesù" or drawing by Correggio
would list generations of owners—the past, as it were,
passed along. When the artifact is ancient as well as of
cultural value (a lion from Sumeria, a burial ornament
from Egypt, a copy of the Magna Carta or the Gold-
berg Variations) it's highly prized and priced. To refor-
mulate Percy Bysshe Shelley's line in "Ozymandias":
"Look on my works, ye mighty, and acquire."

A mantra of the present moment, in terms of our
energy crisis, is that fuel should be "renewable." We
hope to turn from fossil fuels—coal, oil—and harness
a source of energy—solar, or compost, or wind—that
can be renewed. Why should this not be equally a term
applicable to our artistic energy, a way of describing a

form of production that does not grow more costly and has not been depleted at term's end? Admittedly I venture here into the bog of metaphor—where to tread too heavily is soon or late to sink. But it may well prove possible to fashion an aesthetic modeled on the notion of energy saved and transferred.

There was, at one time, a widespread belief in heat as a natural substance: an entity as actual as air. This invisible substance transitioning from site to site was called by scientists "phlogiston." In the late eighteenth century, however, Benjamin Thompson, Count Rumford, disproved the existence of that imagined element and enlarged our understanding of the nature of heat transfer. Instead of a finite thing, *phlogiston*, moving from log to log or hand to cheek, he stipulated that heat was not a quantity which must be by usage reduced. In the history of science, this distinction proved important. It has even been suggested that here was the start of thermodynamics and thereafter the nuclear age: a recognition (well before technology enabled it) that heat was both expansive and renewable, not a thing to be used up.

Again, the analogy beckons; again I offer it cautiously. But it's no accident that most of the elder artists I here discuss are of recent vintage; we use ourselves up less rapidly now and, since the eighteenth century, live longer year by year. Benjamin Thompson established his proof by boring the emperor's cannon in Munich and showing how a pool of cold water in which a can-non's feet rested could be constantly reheated by the metal's transferred heat. Phlogiston—that entity which would have, if finite, been dispersed—could therefore not exist. Instead, as Thompson demonstrated, heat can be engendered by a set of actions that continue to pro-duce. So too I think it feasible that the artistic impulse need not end up depleted but can be renewed.

By and large, moreover, the old creative artist embraces a different set of challenges and new expressive mode. What he may lose in brilliance he gains in objectivity; what she relinquishes in prowess she gains in grasp and reach. It's *adaptative* energy that is entailed in "lastingness," not mere sheer repetition. What these figures seem to seek is less a continually repeating warmth, as in the emperor's foundry, than a fresh source or wellspring of heat.

• • •

So now that I myself approach the delimiting term of this study, and the age of seventy no longer seems far distant, it's time to ask what's lost and what remains. As the list of publications at this text's start will show, I have not been idle. I published my first novel when twenty-three, and this is my twenty-fifth book. *Lasting-ness* will not, I hope, prove to be my final one, but it does feel like a subject I could not have tackled before. To make a splash, an impression, "to become immortal

and then die"—in that coy formulation from Godard's
À Bout de Souffle (1960)—were ambitions earlier; now
what I aspire to is work that will survive.

The youthful exuberance of Delbanco's prose,
moreover, troubles the older Delbanco, who has
learned to admire restraint. The good news—or so I
tell myself—is I'm a better writer today than was the
case to start with; the bad news is the same. Some forty
years ago, in a review of my fourth novel, a critic for the
New York Times declared: "An excellent writer is among
us, and if we neglect him...we shall have to apologize
to posterity."[1] That generous critic, John Leonard, is
dead; his notion of "posterity" is a present audience,
and neglect's a comparative term. What seemed so fas-
cinating to me once—the play of ego on the page, the
clamorous imperatives of rodomontade and katechresis
(read, dear reader, rhetoric)—has latterly felt wasteful,
boastful, and beside the point.

The point, these days, is power-in-reserve. That
task—less energy, more conservation—is, it would seem,
widely shared. This particular artist has attempted to
become less self-referential and more outward focused,
which is why the first-person pronoun has here been
deployed with some care. What signals the art of old age?
How best to equate change and growth? I ask myself
such questions daily; daily I postpone the answer; lately
I have come to see that in the very act of postponement

resides a kind of answer. It's not, perhaps, avoidance so much as acquiescence. The journey not arrival matters; so we learn at journey's end.

A single further memory, and this *me*-moire concludes:

One summer night on Martha's Vineyard in 1967 I was at Max Eastman's house for dinner with two of his friends—the painter Thomas Hart Benton (1889–1975) and the founder of the ACLU, Roger Baldwin (1884–1981). Their wives were elsewhere occupied; I made the fourth of four. Since Eastman then was eighty-four, there were nearly 250 years of accumulated experience lodged in these consequential elders, and I told myself to pay attention: Here was the intersection of visual and verbal art, philosophy and culture, the nexus of much I revered. Benton was a painter of great skill and power, Baldwin a man who organized and supervised a force for social good. The three were still healthy, productive. I knew enough to know how fortunate I was to be included in that company, and while I poured their drinks and cleared their plates I knew I would learn a life lesson: Here were art and literature, personal and civil liberty, politics and activism impressively gathered together.

Benton shouted; Eastman stammered; Baldwin was deaf. They smoked and coughed and swore. As the night wore on and liquor did its playful work, talk turned to old adventures—who'd beat out whom with which red-head or blonde, who'd gone home with which brunette.

They slapped each other's backs. They complained about the weather, tourist traffic on the island, the behavior of their children and neighbors and museum directors and publishers and lawyers; they insulted each other and told bad jokes and dropped the pot of decaffeinated coffee I had so prudently brewed. Wheezing, sneezing, sputtering, they behaved like nothing so much as the college boys I told myself I'd left behind; these *Great Companions*—to use one of Max's titles, though he himself was writing of Einstein, Trotsky, Hemingway, and Freud—had feet of clay up to their necks. "Their ancient, glittering eyes" might well have been, as Yeats wrote, "gay," but over the course of the evening were growing heavy lidded. The revolutionary and painter and reformer—magisterial old masters, each—fell asleep in their soft chairs.

As someday I hope I may too.

• • •

Let me repeat the last three propositions, here, of Chapter One:

The long view and the near are linked: bifocals help.

All young artists have been "promising." Some deliver on that promise and become "distinguished." The trick is to negotiate the forty or the fifty intervening years.

Rarely—very rarely, and yet it still can happen—the final act improves upon the first.

These pages have, I hope, advanced some tentative solutions to the problem posed: How might the "trick" of continuity result in a promise delivered? There's the model of Pablo Casals—who shifted from performance but continued making music—and the model of Giuseppe di Lampedusa, who commenced his book when old. There's Francisco José de Goya y Lucientes, locked into his deafness and apocalyptic vision, who in his eighties fashioned art we now see as prophetic of the present age. There are career trajectories like those of Georgia O'Keeffe and Franz Liszt, who at a certain point withdrew from public view. There's the example of Giuseppe Verdi, who enlarged upon what went before, of Claude Monet, embarking on the project of the *Nymphéas*, and that of William Butler Yeats, whose poetry grew great.

There are those I have referred to only briefly (Leoš Janáček, Walter Savage Landor, Tiziano Vecellio) who persisted in their labors till the end. There are innovative masters like William Shakespeare and Ludwig von Beethoven, dead in their fifties, or Johann Sebastian Bach and Rembrandt van Rijn, dead at sixty-five and sixty-six, who did not reach what we would now call senior status but in their time were old. There are those youthful artists (Keats, Kafka, Mozart, Schubert, Seurat, Van Gogh) whose creative passage through the span of life was quick. There are twenty names to name for every one I've mentioned, and the survey has barely begun. Indeed, *To Be Continued* is this inquiry's clarion call.

It can of course be argued that greatness defies expectation—that by its very nature it violates the norm. But the artists here described personify a kind of staying power we see in non-artists as well; there are many vital "elders" who don't write, compose, or paint. The creative impulse is a common denominator in those who cook or cultivate their gardens, and satisfaction can be found in work never intended for show. It's not, I mean, a sine qua non of productive old age that there be art produced.

When the work as well as the worker can claim lastingness, however, there's a confluence of maker and thing made. "Life force"—that inexact but suggestive phrase—is in this sense renewable, a component part of character that somehow does survive. The majority of figures discussed in this study have tried for, if not constancy, consistency: the daily, weekly, monthly, yearly accretion of what can be seen, read, or heard. And there's something doubly moving in the image of an elder artist, bent to the page or the canvas or score, meditating the next mark. It is a woman walking down a lane in snow, a soldier on his deathbed confessing life-long love. It is contrapuntal voices in a requiem, a dissonance of strings. It is an arrangement of apples, a naked shape emerging from a block of marble. Chill, it still generates heat.

NOTES

INTRODUCTION

1. Barbara Herrnstein Smith, as cited by John Updike, "Late Works," in *Due Considerations* (New York: Alfred A. Knopf, 2007), 51.

CHAPTER ONE. Enemies of Promise

1. Oscar Wilde, *The Critic As Artist* (København: Green Integer, 1997), 97.
2. Oscar Wilde, "The Preface," in *The Complete Works of Oscar Wilde: The Picture of Dorian Gray: The 1890 and 1891 Texts,* ed., Joseph Bristow (Oxford: Oxford University Press, 2005), 168.
3. Dudley Fitts, trans. *Poems from the Greek Anthology* (New York: New Directions, 1956), 108.
4. R.F.C. Hull, trans. "The Stages of Life," in *The Portable Jung,* ed., Joseph Campbell (New York: Viking, 1971), 16–17.
5. Alfred Lord Tennyson, "Merlin and Vivien," in *Idylls of the King*, ed., J. M. Gray (New York: Penguin Classics, 1983).
6. Cyril Connolly, *Enemies of Promise* (Boston: Brown and Little, 1939), 119.

7. Samuel Taylor Coleridge, *Biographia Literaria*, Chapter XIV, in *Samuel Taylor Coleridge: The Major Works* (Oxford University Press, 2009), 314.

8. Edward W. Said, *On Late Style: Music and Literature Against the Grain* (New York: Pantheon Books, 2006).

9. *The Variorum Edition of the Poems of W. B. Yeats* (New York: The Macmillan Co., 1966), "The Spur."

10. David W. Galenson, *Old Masters and Young Geniuses* (Princeton: Princeton University Press, 2006).

11. Michael Doran, ed. *Conversations with Cézanne* (Berkeley: University of California Press, 2001), 163.

12. Alfred H. Barr, Jr. *Picasso* (New York: Museum of Modern Art, 1946), 270.

13. As of the date of this writing (June 2007) a single "Nymphéas" canvas fetched $36.7 million after commission on auction in London; it was sold by the family of a collector who bought it in the 1920s from Monet's son Michel.

CHAPTER TWO. Mere Oblivion

1. This, and much of the subsequent information as to the age of artists, comes from *The Book of Ages: Who Did What When?* by Desmond Morris (New York: Penguin Books, 1985).

2. Deborah Sontag, "At 94, She's the Hot New Thing in Painting," *The New York Times,* December 20, 2009.

3. Much of the data here derives from the *The World Factbook 2007* (Washington, D.C.: Central Intelligence Agency, 2007). Web.

4. This and all other quotations from Shakespeare come from *The Riverside Shakespeare, Second Edition, The Complete Works,* eds., Evans, Tobin et al. (Boston: Houghton Mifflin Co., 1997).

5. Stephen Greenblatt, *Will in the World* (New York: W. W. Norton & Co., 2004), 330.

6. Jack Lynch, *Becoming Shakespeare: The Unlikely Afterlife That Turned a Provincial Playwright into the Bard* (New York: Walker and Co., 2007).

CHAPTER THREE. Brief Long Lives

1. Claire Tomalin, *Thomas Hardy* (New York: The Penguin Press, 2007), 340.
2. Ibid., xxv.
3. *Grove's Dictionary of Music and Musicians*, vol. 2, ed., J. A. Fuller Maitland (New York: The Macmillan Co., 1910), 349.
4. Georg August Griesinger, *Biographical Notes Concerning Joseph Haydn* (1810), reprinted in *Haydn: Two Contemporary Portraits,* ed., Vernon Gotwals (Madison: University of Wisconsin Press, 1968), 17.
5. H. C. Robbins Landon, *Haydn: A Documentary Study* (New York: Rizzoli, 1981), 192–93.
6. René Percheron and Christian Brouder, *Matisse, from Color to Architecture* (New York: Harry N. Abrams, 2004), 326.
7. Alan Wilkinson, ed. *Henry Moore: Writings and Conversations* (Berkeley: University of California Press, 2002), 198.
8. Hall, Donald, "Starting and Keeping On," in *The Hopwood Lectures: Sixth Series,* ed., Nicholas Delbanco (Ann Arbor: University of Michigan Press, 2009), 31.
9. As quoted in Patricia Hills, *Alice Neel* (New York: Harry N. Abrams, Inc., 1983), 185.
10. Ibid., 11.
11. Ibid., 187.
12. Francis Steegmuller and Barbara Bray, trans., *Flaubert-Sand: The Correspondence* (New York: Alfred A. Knopf, 1993), 379.
13. Joseph Barry, *Infamous Woman: The Life of George Sand* (New York: Anchor Books, 1978).
14. Francis Steegmuller and Barbara Bray, trans., *Flaubert-Sand, The Correspondence,* 383.

15. Belinda Jack, *George Sand: A Woman's Wife Writ Large* (London: Chatto & Windus, 1999), 3, 353.

16. Francis Steegmuller and Barbara Bray, trans., *Flaubert-Sand, The Correspondence,* 383.

17. To my mind the best re-creation of that courtship and marriage is the novel by J. D. Landis, *Longing* (New York: Harcourt, Inc., 2000).

18. As quoted in Berthold Litzmann, *Clara Schumann: An Artist's Life, Based on Materials Found in Diaries and Letters.* Vol. 2. Grace E. Hadow, trans. (United States: Litzmann Press, 2007), 36–37.

19. Harold C. Schonberg, "Florestan and Eusebius: Robert Schumann," in *The Lives of the Great Composers* (New York: W. W. Norton, 1997), 176.

20. *Grove's Dictionary of Music and Musicians*, vol. 4, 344.

21. Cathy Porter, trans., *The Diaries of Sophia Tolstoy* (New York: Random House, 1985), 586.

22. Henri Troyat, *Tolstoy,* trans., Nancy Amphoux (Garden City: Doubleday & Company, 1967), 530.

23. Tatyana Tolstoy, *Tolstoy Remembered*, trans., Derek Coltman (London: Michael Joseph, 1977), 128. Caption of a photograph.

24. Frank Stewart Howes, *The Later Works of R. Vaughan Williams* (New York: Oxford University Press, 1937).

25. "Vaughan Williams's Sixth Symphony," *The Times,* Friday, April 30, 1948, 7.

26. Ursula Vaughan Williams. *R.V.W : A Biography of Ralph Vaughan Williams* (New York: Oxford University Press, 1964).

27. John E. Lunn and Ursula Vaughan Williams, *Ralph Vaughan Williams: A Pictorial Biography* (New York: Oxford University Press, 1971).

CHAPTER FOUR. "Each Day I Am Reborn"

1. Michael Hamburger, introduction to *Selected Poems and Fragments* (New York: Penguin Classics, 1998), xxx.
2. William Wordsworth, "Resolution and Independence," in *Selected Poems by William Wordsworth* (New York: Penguin Books, 2004), 139. (He was mourning Thomas Chatterton, a quintessential icon for the romantic poets—young talent gone awry.)
3. Friedrich Hölderlin, *"Das Angenehme Dieser Welt"* in *Friedrich Hölderlin: Poems and Fragments,* ed., Michael Hamburger (London, Routledge and Kegan Paul, 1961), 586; trans., N. Delbanco.
4. Robert Browning, "The Lost Leader," in *The Poetical Works of Robert Browning*, vol. 4 (New York: Oxford University Press, 1991), 56.
5. David Blum, *Casals and the Art of Interpretation* (London: Heinemann Educational Books Ltd., 1977), 50.
6. *Casals, Photographed by Fritz Henle* (Garden City: American Photographic Book Publishing Co., Inc., 1975). Pages are unnumbered.
7. Ibid.
8. Robert Baldock, *Pablo Casals* (London: Victor Gollancz Ltd., 1992), 32.
9. Ibid.
10. *Casals, Photographed by Fritz Henle.*
11. Rudolf Arnheim, "On the Late Style," from *Seasonal Performances, A Michigan Quarterly Review Reader,* ed. Laurence Goldstein (Ann Arbor: The University of Michigan Press, 1991), 119.
12. Lionello. Venturi, ed. *Les Archives de l'impressionisme: Lettres de Renoir, Monet, Pissarro, Sisley et autres: Memoirs de Paul Durand-Ruel* (New York: Burt Franklin, 1968), Letter 1832.

13. L. C. Perry, "Reminiscences of Claude Monet," *American Magazine of Art,* March 18, 1926, 120.

14. Lisel Mueller, "Monet Refuses the Operation," in *A Second Language* (Baton Rouge: Louisiana State University Press, 1986), 59.

15. François Thiébault-Sisson, *"Les Nymphéas de Claude Monet à l'Orangerie,"* in *La revue de l'art ancient et moderne,* June 1927: 48, as cited in Karin Sagner-Düchting, *Monet at Giverny* (New York: Prestel Publishing, 1994), 78.

CHAPTER FIVE. "My Muse Is Young"

1. Leo Janis, "Georgia O'Keeffe at Eighty-Four," *Atlantic Monthly,* December, 1971: 114–17.

2. Ibid.

3. Henry Seldis, "Georgia O'Keeffe at 78: Tough-Minded Romantic," *Los Angeles Times, West Magazine,* January 22, 1967: 22.

4. Lee Nordness, *Art USA Now* (Lucerne, Switzerland: C. J. Bucher, 1962).

5. Letter from O'Keeffe to Stieglitz, July 29, 1937, 1937–38 exhibition catalogue, An American Place, December 27, 1937, to February 11, 1938, as quoted in Laurie Lisle, *Portrait of an Artist* (Albuquerque, University of New Mexico, 1986), 238.

6. Letter from O'Keeffe to Stieglitz, August 16, 1937. Ibid.

7. Daniel Catton Rich, *Georgia O'Keeffe* (Chicago: Art Institute of Chicago, 1943), 316–17.

8. The quotations from his poetry, except where noted, come from *The Variorum Edition of the Poems of W. B. Yeats* (New York: The Macmillan Co., 1966).

9. *The Autobiography of William Butler Yeats* (New York: The Macmillan Co., 1953), 325.

10. This punctuation mirrors that of *The Monthly Review,* December 1902.

11. William Butler Yeats, *A Vision,* revised edition (New York: Macmillan and Company, 1956), 279–280.

12. Anthony Storr, *Solitude: A Return to the Self* (New York, Free Press, 2005), 174–75.

13. Humphrey Searle, *The Music of Liszt* (New York: Dover, 1966), 108.

14. Alan Walker, *Franz Liszt: The Final Years* (New York, Alfred A. Knopf, 1966), 403–404.

15. Carl Lachmund, *Mein Leben mit Franz Liszt* (Eschwege: Schroder, 1970), 247–248, as quoted in Adrian Williams, ed., *Portrait of Liszt* (Oxford: Clarendon Press, 1990), 626.

16. Sacheverell Sitwell, *Liszt* (London: Cassell & Co., Ltd., 1955), 305.

17. La Mara, ed., *Franz Liszt's Briefe,* vol. 2, 389, as quoted in Alan Walker, *Franz Liszt: The Final Years.*

18. Alan Walker, *Franz Liszt: The Final Years,* 506.

CHAPTER SIX. "If We Want Things to Stay as They Are..."

1. Mary Jane Phillips-Matz, *Verdi, A Biography* (New York: Oxford University Press, 1993), 765.

2. For a fuller analysis of the musical techniques and structure of *Falstaff,* see James A. Hepokoski's *Giuseppe Verdi, Falstaff,* (London: Cambridge University Press, 1983), to which I am indebted. This particular quotation comes from p. 96.

3. George Martin, *Verdi, His Music, Life and Times* (New York: Dodd, Mead & Co., 1963), 551.

4. Marcello Conati, ed. *Interviews and Encounters with Verdi,* trans., Richard Stokes (London: Victor Gollancz, Ltd., 1984), xxiii.

5. Felix Philippi, "A Meeting with Verdi," in Marcello Conati, ed., *Interviews and Encounters with Verdi,* 330.

6. George Martin, *Verdi: His Music, Life and Times,* 301.

7. Juan José Junquera, *The Black Paintings of Goya* (London: Scala Publishers, Ltd., 2003), 14.
8. Sánchez Cantón, as quoted in Evan S. Connell, *Francisco Goya: A Life* (New York: Counterpoint, 2004), 214.
9. Robert Motherwell, as quoted in Juan José Junquera, *The Black Paintings of Goya,* 92.
10. As quoted in Connell, *Francisco Goya: A Life*, 123.
11. Antonina Vallentin, *This I Saw: The Life and Times of Goya,* trans., Katherine Woods (New York: Random House, 1949), 317–318.
12. Much of the biographical information here provided comes from David Gilmour, *The Last Leopard: A Life of Giuseppe di Lampedusa* (New York: Quartet Books, 1988), 91.
13. Ibid., 158.
14. Ibid., 162.
15. Letter to Guido Lajolo, March 31, 1956, as cited in Gilmour, 163.
16. *Litteratura Inglese, III,* cited in Gilmour, 106.
17. David Gilmour, *The Last Leopard*, 108.
18. Giuseppe Tomasi di Lampedusa, *The Siren and Selected Writings* (London: The Harvill Press, 1995), 123.
19. David Gilmour, *The Last Leopard*, 128.
20. Giuseppe Tomasi di Lampedusa, *The Siren and Selected Writings,* 13–14.

CHAPTER SEVEN. The Idea of Continuity

1. From the outline for *Brain Fitness* (unpublished), Michael M. Merzenich, Chapter 7.
2. This information is culled from "The Brain, A User's Guide," a "Mind and Body Special Issue" of *Time* Magazine, January 29, 2007, 86–88.
3. James Hillman, *The Force of Character* (New York: Random House, 1999), 3–4.
4. Ibid., 42.

5. *Illustrated Oxford Dictionary* (New York: Oxford University Press, 1998).
6. John Richardson quoted in Carol Vogel, "A Personal Lesson in Late-Period Picasso," *The New York Times,* March 26, 2009.
7. Nicholas Delbanco, *The Lost Suitcase* (New York: Columbia University Press, 2000), 163–64.

CHAPTER EIGHT. Gratification

1. Anthony Storr, *Solitude: A Return to the Self* (New York: The Free Press, 2005), 153–54.
2. Sherwin B. Nuland, *The Art of Aging* (New York: Random House, 2007), 251–252.
3. Ronald Manheimer, *A Map to the End of Time* (New York: W. W. Norton & Co., 1999), 135.
4. Rudolf Arnheim, "On the Late Style," from *Seasonal Performances: A Michigan Quarterly Review Reader,* ed., Laurence Goldstein (Ann Arbor: The University of Michigan Press, 1991), 111.
5. Letter from John Updike to Nicholas Delbanco, August 26, 2007. The essay on "Late Works" to which he refers was first published in *The New Yorker* and included in his *Due Considerations: Essays and Criticism* (New York: Alfred A. Knopf, 2007).
6. *Dear Theo: the Autobiography of Vincent van Gogh,* eds., Irving and Jean Stone, (New York: Grove Press, 1960), 415.
7. *Grove's Dictionary of Music and Musicians,* vol. 1, (New York: The Macmillan Co., 1910), 149.
8. Christoph Wolff, *Johann Sebastian Bach: The Learned Musician* (New York: W. W. Norton & Co., 2000), 433.

CONCLUSION

1. *The New York Times,* Review by John Leonard, June 12, 1970.